# Designs for Cooperative Interactions

Robin Fogarty

Arlington Heights, Illinois

**Designs for Cooperative Interactions**

Published by SkyLight Professional Development
2626 S. Clearbrook Dr., Arlington Heights, IL 60005-5310
800-348-4474 or 847-290-6600
Fax 847-290-6609
info@skylightedu.com
http://www.skylightedu.com

Editing: Sharon Nowakowski
Type Composition: Donna Ramirez
Book Design and Typesetting: Bruce Leckie
Illustration: David Stockman



ISBN 0-932935-28-1

1106-V
Item No. 0628
Z Y X W V U T S R Q P O N M L K J I H G F
06 05 04 03 02 01 00 99 15 14 13 12 11 10 9 8

# DESIGNS FOR COOPERATIVE INTERACTIONS
## ABSTRACT

Ushered in by the global models of cooperation in business and industry, *Designs for Cooperative Interactions* presents 12 practical and proven strategies for the kindergarten to college classroom. A brief introduction provides guidelines for teachers to use this book as a learning tool. Included among the interactive designs are models that become increasingly engaging for the students.

Models range from *Rhetorical Questions* and informal *Turn To Your Partner And . . .* strategies, to physically involving models such as the *Traveling Clusters* in the *People Search* and a *Total Group Response* strategy called the *Human Graph.*

Each model is introduced with a full description. Two-page prompts cue teachers to a classroom vignette that illustrate the student-to-student, student-to-teacher interactions which define the model. Following each design, space is provided for teachers to plan an application, describe the actual lesson and reflect on the results.

The book ends with a summary chart of the models and the representative symbols of the interactions for ready reference. A glimpse at the future school, with its shift toward a more interactive paradigm, concludes the discussion.

# TABLE OF CONTENTS

# FOREWORD

## Designs for Cooperative Interactions:

*On a Planetary Scale*, Buckminster Fuller coins the phrase "Spaceship Earth" as he envisions his concept of a global community, cooperating and co-existing in mutually benefiting ways.

*On a World Scale*, Marilyn Ferguson writes about grass-roots networks conspiring in interwoven cooperative efforts toward societal transformation.

*On an International Scale*, the Japanese skillfully adapt and refine the highly effective participatory model of management called Quality Circles, which spirals cooperative decision-making through every corporate level.

*On an Educational Scale*, Roger and David Johnson elaborate on structured interaction in the classroom. Their research on "circles of learning" outlines a highly feasible cooperative group model for classrooms to increase student achievement and enhance self-concepts.

*On a Personal Scale,* teachers throughout our schools design the new school lecture, using strategies of participation and interaction to engage students cooperatively and thoughtfully.

# PREFACE

## From Lecturer to Learner

From kindergarten classrooms to college lecture halls, educators are moving toward more involving models of instruction. As architects of the intellect, teachers are designing the new school "lecture." In essence, this new "lecture" does not resemble the old lecture very much. In fact, the new "lecture" is really a myriad of interaction patterns. The authentic interaction designs of the new lecture take the focus off the lecturer and put it squarely on the learner. The emergence of the new school lecture is unmistakable.

The gallery of submissions for cooperative designs begins with the traditional stand-up-teaching model of the distinguished lecturer. In this model the learner is viewed as the vessel to be filled. At the other end of the gallery of submissions is the total group involvement model called the human graph in which students physically move along a life-size graph to symbolize their positions on issues.

The shift from the most didactic teaching models to intensely involving designs is no easy task for teachers. Just as in any paradigm shift, major philosophical underpinnings are shaken. Yet, the move toward the new school lecture, with its accent on student interactions, is made easier if seen as a gradual change. Student involvement in lesson activities can be designed so that strategies increase student participation by degrees. In this way, teachers and students can adjust and adapt to the new model over time.

Today, many people picture classroom teaching as teachers standing in front of their classes—teaching! To update that picture and to move toward the new lecture image in which the students are as active as the teacher, schools must approach the change gingerly. When introduced gradually, interactive models provide paradigm shifts for teachers, students and parents.

Surprisingly, however, and almost unfailingly, once the philosophical shift begins; once teachers begin with the cooperative interactions, the evidence of increased student motivation becomes so overwhelmingly visible that teachers are extrinsically encouraged to try more. As the successes of the new interactions take off, the momentum builds for the teachers and the students. Before long, the new school "lecture" becomes the norm. The novelty of the designs is no longer the challenge. The challenge comes in choosing the most appropriate interactive designs for the target lesson—choosing a design in which the final focus rests on the learner, not on the lecturer.

Robin Fogarty
Chicago, Illinois
1990

# INTRODUCTION

## An Overview of 12 Cooperative Interaction Designs

The many variables that come into play as teachers select the most appropriate interactive designs for their lessons include time, physical space, facilities, level and behavior of students, number of students, purpose of the lesson, background and experiences of the students, support materials, teacher expertise and innumerable other considerations.

In the high-content, high-support, high-challenge classroom, the overriding goals are intense student involvement and the transfer of learning into life situations. *High content* refers to standard disciplines such as the sciences, the humanities and the arts; *high support* cites the expectation for cooperative interactions; and *high challenge* dictates the need for meaningful and thoughtful learner activities.

By accumulating a repertoire of interactive designs and coupling the student involvement with information-processing models, the skillful teacher moves

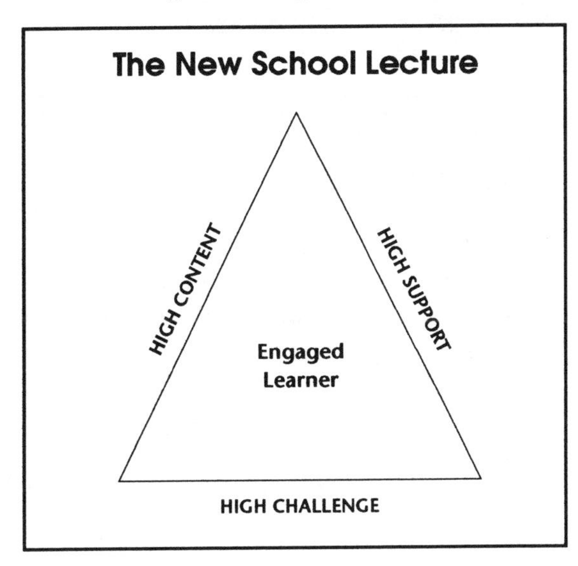

learning for all students into new depths.

As the skilled teacher weighs the variables and surveys the various designs, a particular interaction model or a combination of several emerges as more appropriate than the others. Equipped with these "variations on the theme" of involving students in interactive ways, the skilled teacher readily selects the model from a repertoire such as the following:

| AN OVERVIEW: INTERACTIVE DESIGNS | | |
|---|---|---|
| 1 | Lecture/Rhetorical Questioning: Teacher Talk |  |
| 2 | Signals/Direct Questioning: Surveying | 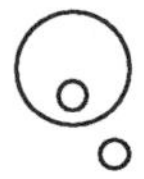 |
| 3 | Turn To Your Partner And . . . TTYPA |  |
| 4 | Paired Partners: Talk Aloud |  |
| 5 | Dyads: Think/Pair/Share |  |
| 6 | Triads: Observer Feedback |  |
| 7 | Tell/Retell: 2-4-8 |  |
| 8 | Cooperative Learning: Groups |  |
| 9 | Traveling Clusters: People Search | 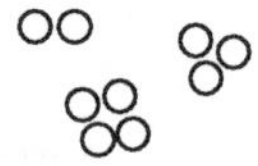 |
| 10 | Forced Response: Wraparound |  |
| 11 | Total Group Response: Human Graph | 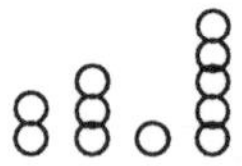 |
| 12 | Group Investigation: Jigsaw | 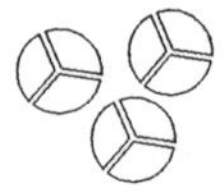 |

Each of the classroom interaction designs uses a different degree of student involvement. The designs at the top of the chart, such as *Lecture/Rhetorical Questioning*, require minimal learner participation while the designs at the bottom, such as *Cooperative Learning: Groups* and *Forced Response*, engage learners intensely by the very nature and structure of their strategies.

## A Look at the Designs

Each of the 12 designs is introduced for easy application to any classroom situation. Beginning with a *quote* and a *one-page description* of a design, each introduction also includes a **Source** for whom the author credits the foundations of the design.

Adjacent to the one-page description, is a quick reference page for teachers to easily refer to when deciding upon the right design for each lesson. The reference page offers a **Prescription** for when the design would be appropriate to use. The *symbol* on the chalkboard offers a visual reminder of the design and its components that structure student interaction. Since the 12 interactive models work well with all levels—elementary, middle, high school, college—all of the levels are modeled in at least one **Description**. Teachers may need to make moderate adjustments to the designs when tailoring them to the age level and content of their classes. The **Vignette** provides a brief illustration of the interactive design as set up in the **Description**. The brief **Notes** are metacognitive cues or labels that clarify the actions in the vignette. (See the sample below.)

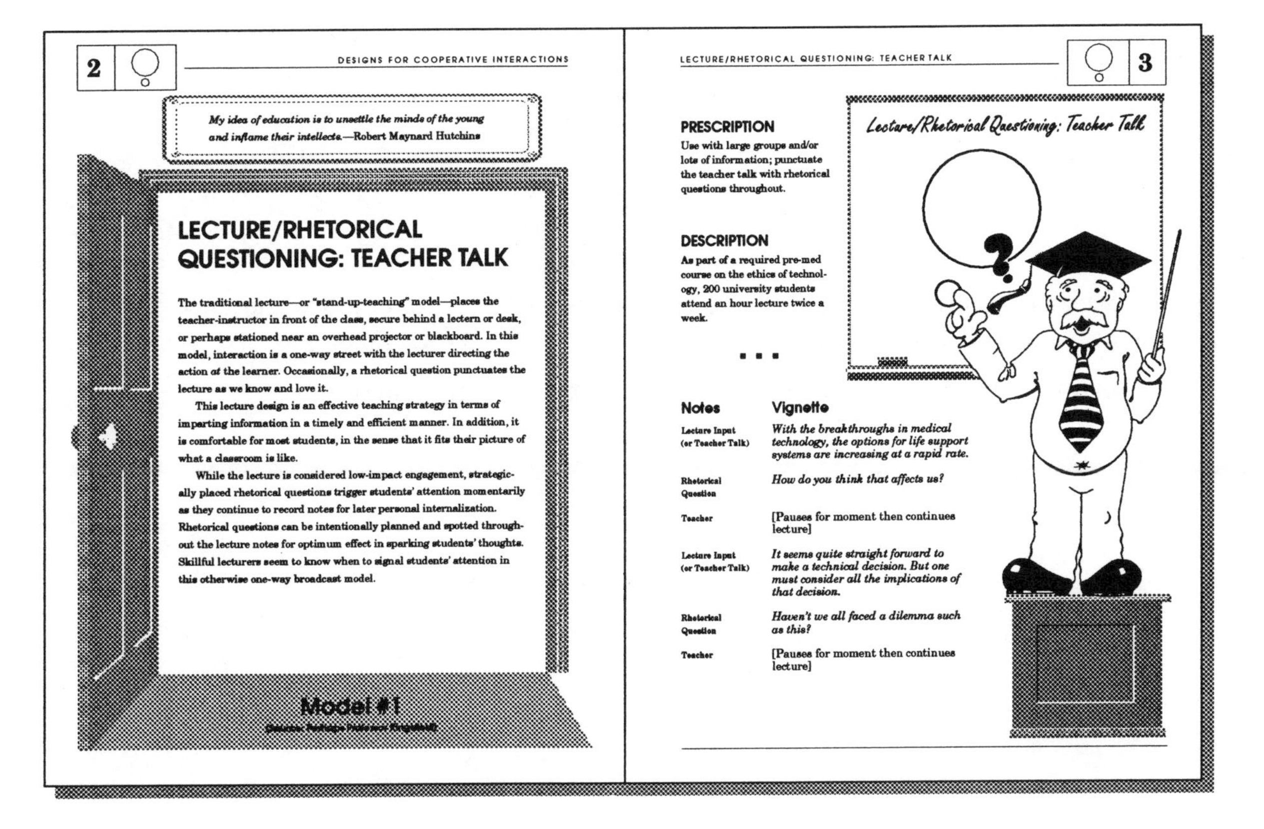

2 DESIGNS FOR COOPERATIVE INTERACTIONS

*My idea of education is to unsettle the minds of the young and inflame their intellects.*—Robert Maynard Hutchins

**LECTURE/RHETORICAL QUESTIONING: TEACHER TALK**

The traditional lecture—or "stand-up-teaching" model—places the teacher-instructor in front of the class, secure behind a lectern or desk, or perhaps stationed near an overhead projector or blackboard. In this model, interaction is a one-way street with the lecturer directing the action *at* the learner. Occasionally, a rhetorical question punctuates the lecture as we know and love it.

This lecture design is an effective teaching strategy in terms of imparting information in a timely and efficient manner. In addition, it is comfortable for most students, in the sense that it fits their picture of what a classroom is like.

While the lecture is considered low-impact engagement, strategically placed rhetorical questions trigger students' attention momentarily as they continue to record notes for later personal internalization. Rhetorical questions can be intentionally planned and spotted throughout the lecture notes for optimum effect in sparking students' thoughts. Skillful lecturers seem to know when to signal students' attention in this otherwise one-way broadcast model.

Model #1

LECTURE/RHETORICAL QUESTIONING: TEACHER TALK 3

**PRESCRIPTION**

Use with large groups and/or lots of information; punctuate the teacher talk with rhetorical questions throughout.

**DESCRIPTION**

As part of a required pre-med course on the ethics of technology, 200 university students attend an hour lecture twice a week.

■ ■ ■



| Notes | Vignette |
| --- | --- |
| Lecture Input (or Teacher Talk) | *With the breakthroughs in medical technology, the options for life support systems are increasing at a rapid rate.* |
| Rhetorical Question | *How do you think that affects us?* |
| Teacher | [Pauses for moment then continues lecture] |
| Lecture Input (or Teacher Talk) | *It seems quite straight forward to make a technical decision. But one must consider all the implications of that decision.* |
| Rhetorical Question | *Haven't we all faced a dilemma such as this?* |
| Teacher | [Pauses for moment then continues lecture] |

## How to Use this Book

To use this book of interactive designs most effectively, a four-step approach seems appropriate.

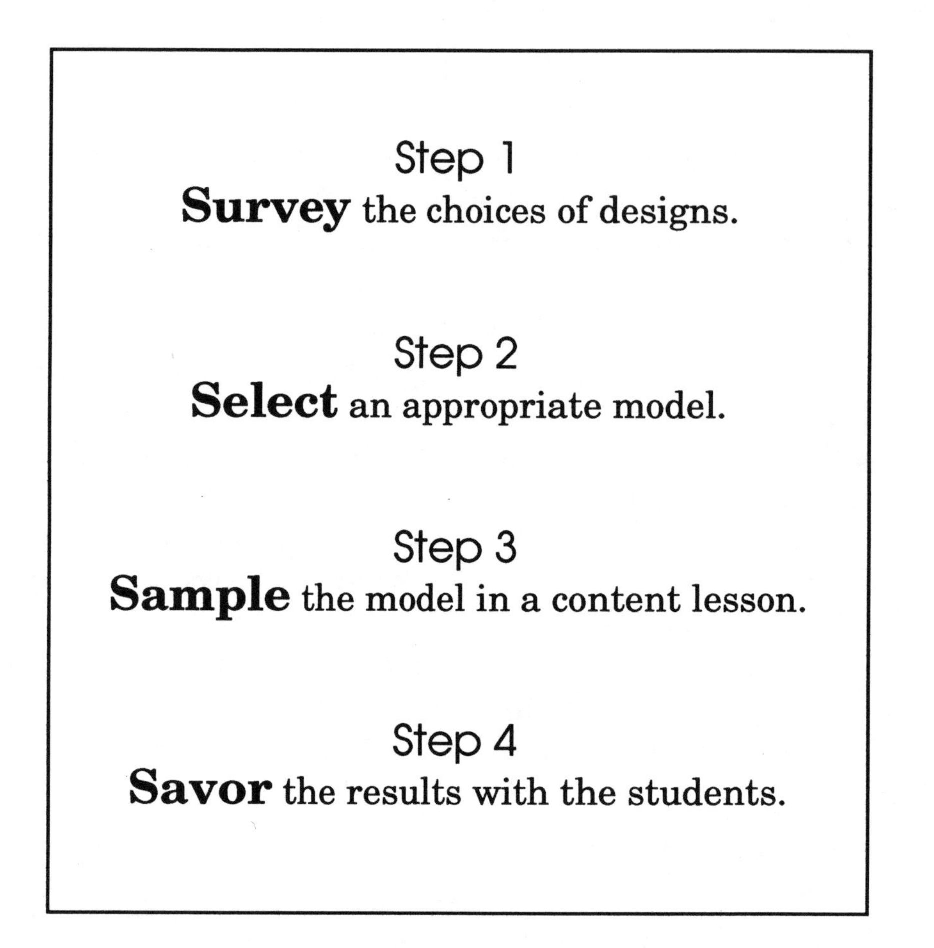


**Survey:** Using the chart on the next page, *survey* and explore the various designs for cooperative interactions. Then, turn to the new school lecture designs and learn more about their varying degrees of interaction.

| DESIGN | EXPLANATION |
| --- | --- |
| Lecture/Rhetorical Questioning: Teacher Talk | Stand-up teaching; lecturing to whole class. |
| Signals/Direct Questioning: Surveying | Lecturing to class; interrupting with signals by group or for answer by one student. |
| Turn To Your Partner And . . .: TTYPA | Informal sharing by partners in which interaction is brief and quick. |
| Paired Partners: Talk Alouds | One partner reflecting the thinking of the other partner who is talking aloud as he thinks through a problem. |
| Dyads: Think/Pair/Share | Partners first thinking alone and then sharing ideas—sometimes coming to one idea for their pair. |
| Triads: Observer Feedback | Partner interaction enhanced by objective observer feedback. |
| Tell–Retell: 2-4-8 | Two people telling ideas; two sets of two retelling their partners' ideas; a group of eight retelling all ideas. |
| Cooperative Learning: Groups | Small groups of three or four students working interdependently, but all members accountable for all the work. |
| Traveling Clusters: People Search | Students moving from group to group, forming informal clusters as they share information and gather signatures. |
| Forced Response: Wrap Around | Round-robin style, students responding in turn to a lead-in statement cued by the teacher. |
| Total Group Response: Human Graph | Students lining up on an imaginary graph to indicate their preferences. |
| Group Investigation: Jigsaw | In groups of three, each member researching a third of its group's work and then teaching it to the other members. |

**Select:** To select an appropriate design, determine the *purpose* of the lesson. Then, target the design most helpful for achieving the desired outcome. For example, if the purpose is to get a grasp of a new concept, a *Turn To Your Partner And . . .* might be the best approach for a quick processing of the idea and anchoring of that idea through partner articulation.

**Sample:** Once a design is selected, *sample* it in a content lesson. To introduce students to the new strategy, give the design explicit attention as part of the content of the lesson. Let students sample the interaction methodology as well as the subject content. Prior to the lesson, use the lesson planner pages accompanying each design to sketch a lesson application. Begin in the left-hand column with the Think Abouts. Then sketch your ideas on the right-hand side under My Lesson Idea.

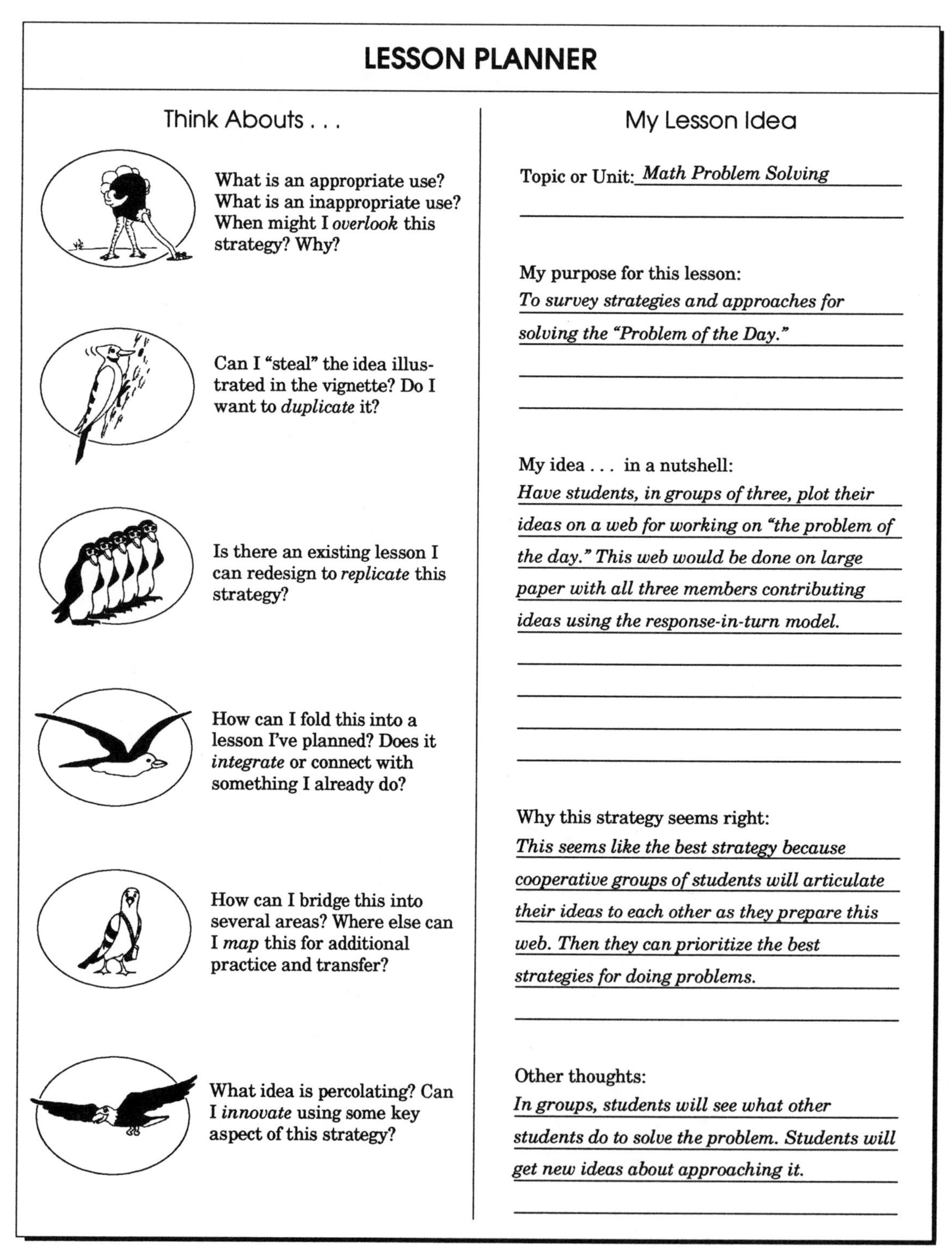

**LESSON PLANNER**

| Think Abouts . . . | My Lesson Idea |
|---|---|
| What is an appropriate use? What is an inappropriate use? When might I *overlook* this strategy? Why? | Topic or Unit: *Math Problem Solving*<br><br>My purpose for this lesson:<br>*To survey strategies and approaches for solving the "Problem of the Day."* |
| Can I "steal" the idea illustrated in the vignette? Do I want to *duplicate* it? | |
| Is there an existing lesson I can redesign to *replicate* this strategy? | My idea . . . in a nutshell:<br>*Have students, in groups of three, plot their ideas on a web for working on "the problem of the day." This web would be done on large paper with all three members contributing ideas using the response-in-turn model.* |
| How can I fold this into a lesson I've planned? Does it *integrate* or connect with something I already do? | |
| How can I bridge this into several areas? Where else can I *map* this for additional practice and transfer? | Why this strategy seems right:<br>*This seems like the best strategy because cooperative groups of students will articulate their ideas to each other as they prepare this web. Then they can prioritize the best strategies for doing problems.* |
| What idea is percolating? Can I *innovate* using some key aspect of this strategy? | Other thoughts:<br>*In groups, students will see what other students do to solve the problem. Students will get new ideas about approaching it.* |

**Savor:** After the lesson, *savor* the student outcomes of the selected and sampled design by deliberately processing the material and focusing on the interaction itself. Elicit feedback to evaluate the interactive methodology. Use the double-entry journal pages provided after each design to reflect upon the application lesson. Complete the descriptions in the first column immediately following the lessons. Then, at a later date, reflect upon those descriptions in the second column.

## DOUBLE-ENTRY JOURNAL: PROCESSING

| Description of the Lesson | Reflections on the Lesson |
|---|---|
| What I did before the lesson:<br>*In the groups, I planned for a recorder, a reporter, and a materials manager. Also, I had large paper, markers, and tape. Students were grouped by ability—low, middle, and high. I used the task groups from last week.* | Thoughts, ideas, connections I'm making . . .<br><br>*Yesterday's webs are still hanging on the walls. In looking them over, I am amazed at the diversity of them.*<br><br>*The cooperative group model really worked well. It got kids talking about and recording their ideas. The conversations were lively and I felt like kids did get some new ideas.*<br><br>*I think I'll do a log entry and a wraparound today to see just what ideas really stuck with them. Then I'll encourage them to try a new approach today—in partners—for the problem. The partnership may help them take more risks.* |
| What I did during the lesson:<br>*The "webs" seemed more elaborate than I was expecting. I think I should have talked about the "mapping" of information as compared to "a web of attributes." But, I needed to plan that before I approached it with students.* | |
| What I did following the lesson:<br>*As students shared their strategies for attacking the problem of the day, I think they were surprised at the number of different ways people approach a solution. There were lots of ideas about representing the information graphically.* | |

## How to Use this Book Repeatedly—A Word About Transfer

Contrary to popular opinion, the teaching of Latin does not necessarily transfer by "training the mind," just as the study of geometry does not automatically transfer into the "learning of logic." While teaching general heuristics such as math problem-solving may result in the use of the strategies under the watchful eye of the math teacher, the same heuristics do not seem to transfer into problem-solving steps for the writing process. Transfer does not seem to occur unshepherded in the natural course of the learning process.

Current transfer theory suggests, however, that when we pay attention to transfer in contextual learning situations, transfer does indeed occur. And, when general bare strategies are accompanied with self-monitoring techniques, again, transfer does in fact occur. In essence, when transfer is guided and mediated, transfer happens. This "good shepherd theory" (1990 Perkins) suggests that when provoked, practiced and reflected upon, transfer is fairly easy to get.

Salomon and Perkins refer to "lowroad" automatic transfer and "highroad" abstract transfer. They further describe two mediation strategies for lowroad and highroad transfer which they label "hugging and bridging."

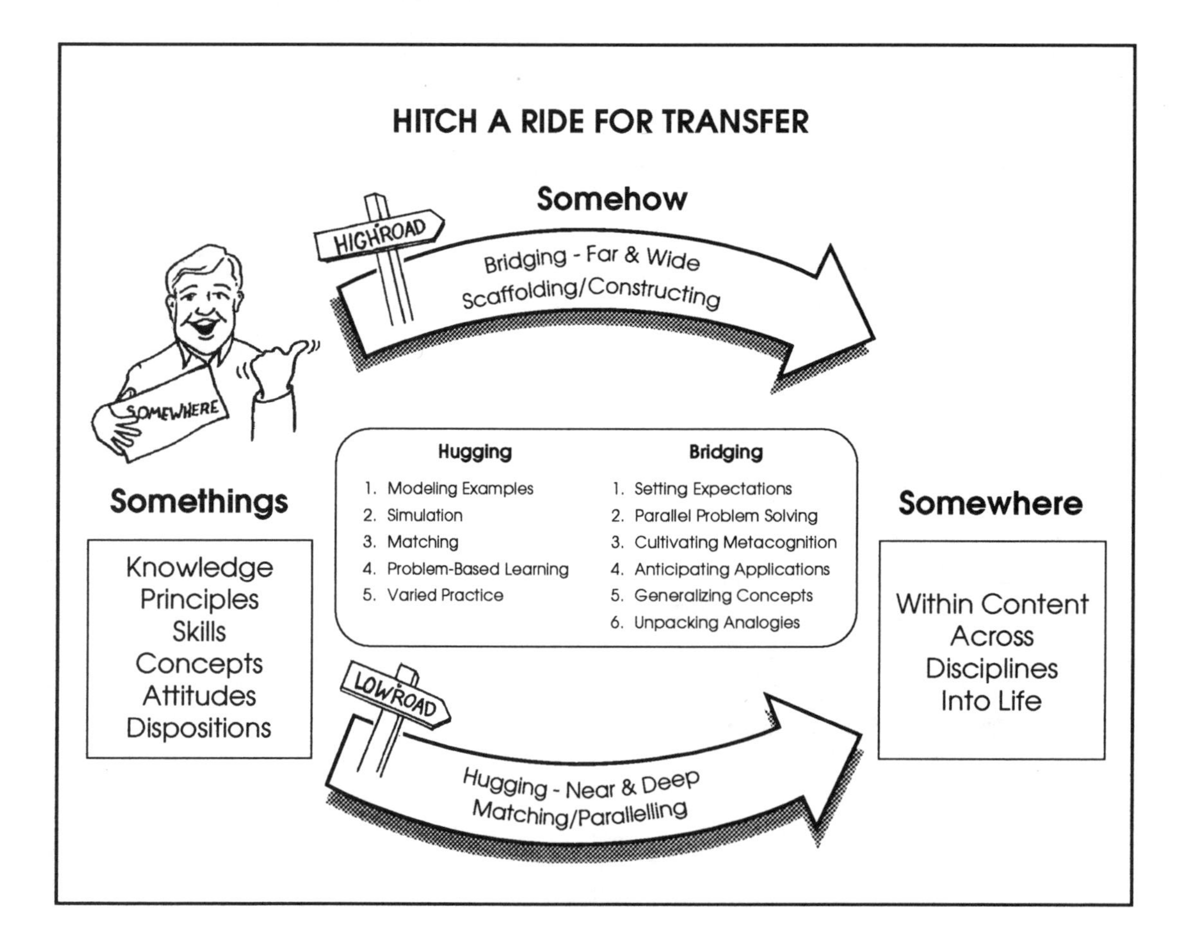

"Hugging means teaching so as to better meet the resemblance conditions for lowroad or "automatic" transfer. Bridging means teaching to better meet the conditions for highroad transfer by mediating the needed processes of abstraction and connection making."

Beyer refers to mediation as cuing. We can cue learners about what to do, when it's appropriate and how to do it.

Perkins further suggests that teachers use both anticipatory tactics and retrieval tactics to promote transfer. The following categories are suggested:

| TRANSFER TACTICS | |
|---|---|
| ANTICIPATORY | RETRIEVAL |
| **Highroad** - abstracting rules<br>- anticipating applications | - reflecting by generalizing the problem<br>- focusing retrieval in one particular context<br>- making metaphors |
| **Lowroad** - practicing immediately<br>- varying practice<br>- matching lesson to target | - spacing and varying practice over time |

In addition, Joyce and Showers suggest that while horizontal transfer shifts directly, vertical transfer requires adaptation to fit the new conditions. High transfer requires understanding of the purpose and rationale of the skill and know-how to adapt it skillfully.

Fogarty suggests a continuum of transfer behavior within the dichotomy of simple and complex transfer. The learner levels, originally indicative of adult creative transfer are similarly applied to student transfer as depicted on the charts on the following pages.

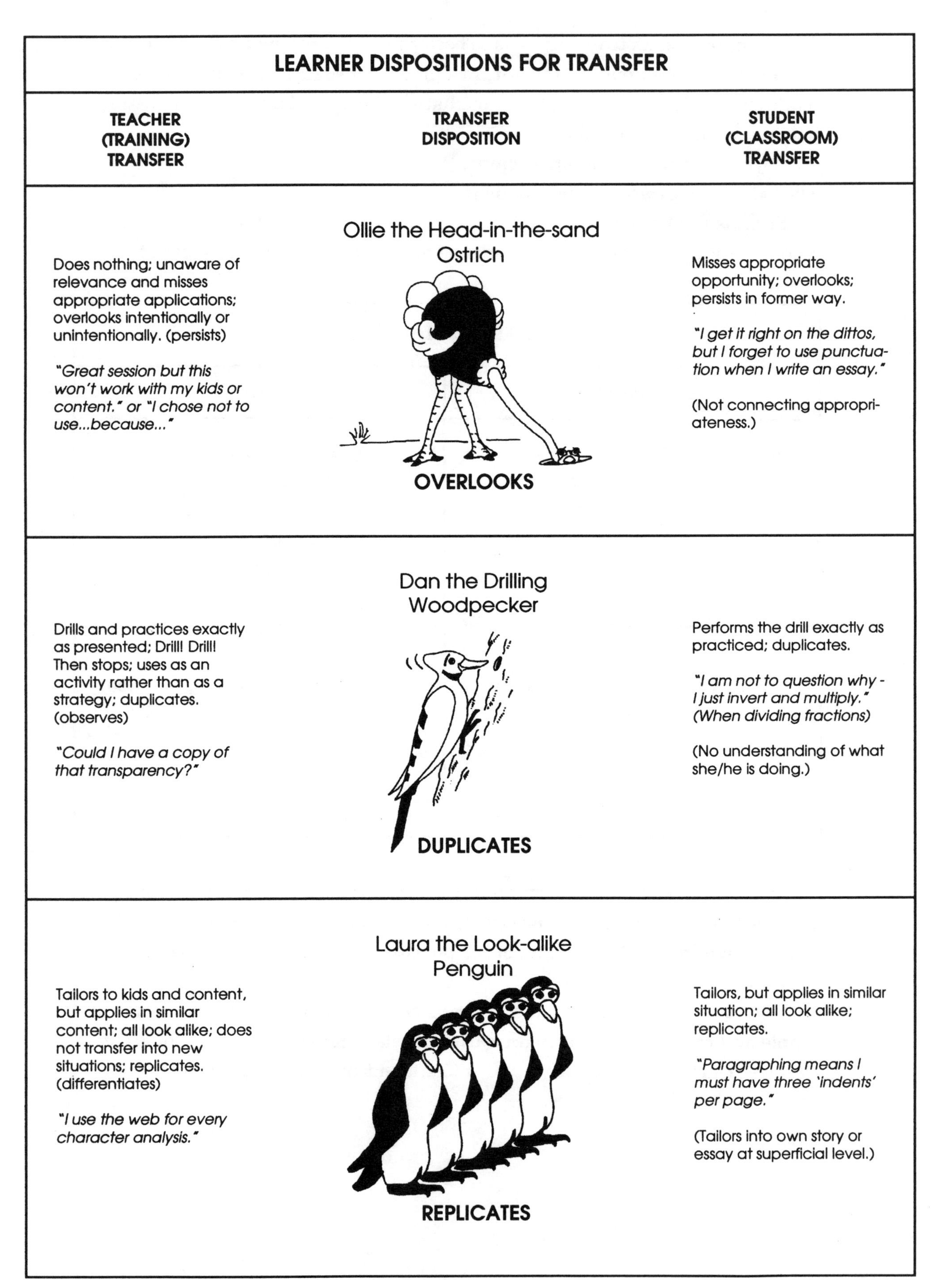

**LEARNER DISPOSITIONS FOR TRANSFER**

| TEACHER (TRAINING) TRANSFER | TRANSFER DISPOSITION | STUDENT (CLASSROOM) TRANSFER |
|---|---|---|
| Does nothing; unaware of relevance and misses appropriate applications; overlooks intentionally or unintentionally. (persists)<br><br>*"Great session but this won't work with my kids or content." or "I chose not to use...because..."* | Ollie the Head-in-the-sand Ostrich<br><br>**OVERLOOKS** | Misses appropriate opportunity; overlooks; persists in former way.<br><br>*"I get it right on the dittos, but I forget to use punctuation when I write an essay."*<br><br>(Not connecting appropriateness.) |
| Drills and practices exactly as presented; Drill! Drill! Then stops; uses as an activity rather than as a strategy; duplicates. (observes)<br><br>*"Could I have a copy of that transparency?"* | Dan the Drilling Woodpecker<br><br>**DUPLICATES** | Performs the drill exactly as practiced; duplicates.<br><br>*"I am not to question why - I just invert and multiply." (When dividing fractions)*<br><br>(No understanding of what she/he is doing.) |
| Tailors to kids and content, but applies in similar content; all look alike; does not transfer into new situations; replicates. (differentiates)<br><br>*"I use the web for every character analysis."* | Laura the Look-alike Penguin<br><br>**REPLICATES** | Tailors, but applies in similar situation; all look alike; replicates.<br><br>*"Paragraphing means I must have three 'indents' per page."*<br><br>(Tailors into own story or essay at superficial level.) |

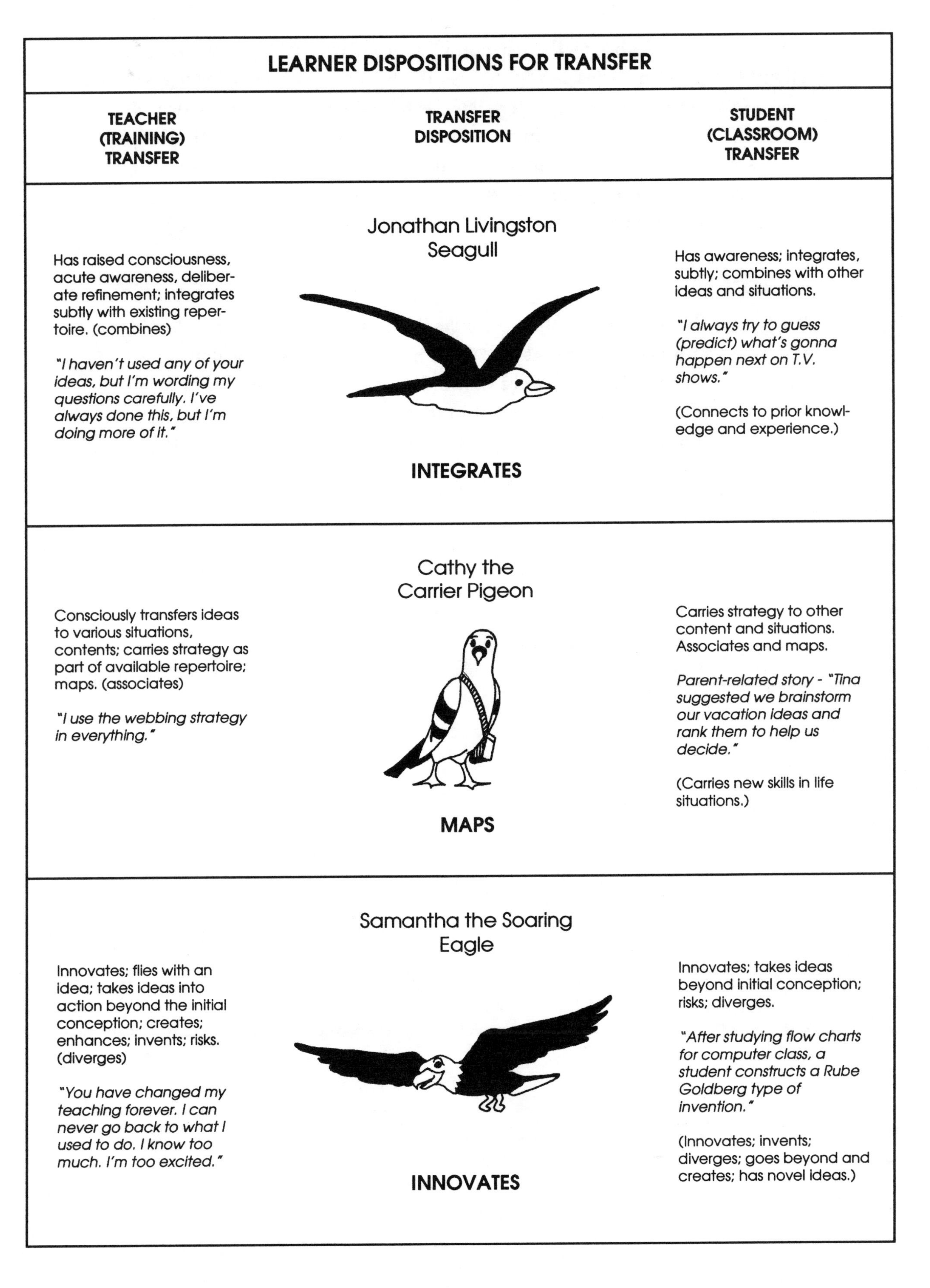

**LEARNER DISPOSITIONS FOR TRANSFER**

| TEACHER (TRAINING) TRANSFER | TRANSFER DISPOSITION | STUDENT (CLASSROOM) TRANSFER |
|---|---|---|
| Has raised consciousness, acute awareness, deliberate refinement; integrates subtly with existing repertoire. (combines)<br><br>*"I haven't used any of your ideas, but I'm wording my questions carefully. I've always done this, but I'm doing more of it."* | Jonathan Livingston Seagull<br><br>**INTEGRATES** | Has awareness; integrates, subtly; combines with other ideas and situations.<br><br>*"I always try to guess (predict) what's gonna happen next on T.V. shows."*<br><br>(Connects to prior knowledge and experience.) |
| Consciously transfers ideas to various situations, contents; carries strategy as part of available repertoire; maps. (associates)<br><br>*"I use the webbing strategy in everything."* | Cathy the Carrier Pigeon<br><br>**MAPS** | Carries strategy to other content and situations. Associates and maps.<br><br>*Parent-related story - "Tina suggested we brainstorm our vacation ideas and rank them to help us decide."*<br><br>(Carries new skills in life situations.) |
| Innovates; flies with an idea; takes ideas into action beyond the initial conception; creates; enhances; invents; risks. (diverges)<br><br>*"You have changed my teaching forever. I can never go back to what I used to do. I know too much. I'm too excited."* | Samantha the Soaring Eagle<br><br>**INNOVATES** | Innovates; takes ideas beyond initial conception; risks; diverges.<br><br>*"After studying flow charts for computer class, a student constructs a Rube Goldberg type of invention."*<br><br>(Innovates; invents; diverges; goes beyond and creates; has novel ideas.) |

If an idea is used once by the teacher, it is an activity. If that same idea is used repeatedly with variations on the theme, the idea becomes a strategy, a tool to add to the teacher's bag of tricks. By establishing an increased awareness of transfer and by using cuing questions to mediate transfer, activities can become strategies. It is the intent of the author to facilitate lasting transfer by using these designs as strategies, over and over again, whenever they seem appropriate to the teaching situation.

## One Last Note

Initially, the skilled teacher subtly slots the designs into the lessons to familiarize students with the different interactions and to lead them toward involvement in the learning situation. Once the various designs have been introduced, and as the students become more adept in their social skills, the teacher selects models according to their appropriateness for the overriding purpose of the lesson.

*Freedom of inquiry, freedom of discussion and freedom of teaching—without these a university cannot exist.*—Robert Maynard Hutchins
THE NEW SCHOOL LECTURE

*My idea of education is to unsettle the minds of the young and inflame their intellects.*—Robert Maynard Hutchins

# LECTURE/RHETORICAL QUESTIONING: TEACHER TALK

The traditional lecture—or "stand-up-teaching" model—places the teacher-instructor in front of the class, secure behind a lectern or desk, or perhaps stationed near an overhead projector or blackboard. In this model, interaction is a one-way street with the lecturer directing the action *at* the learner. Occasionally, a rhetorical question punctuates the lecture as we know and love it.

This lecture design is an effective teaching strategy in terms of imparting information in a timely and efficient manner. In addition, it is comfortable for most students, in the sense that it fits their picture of what a classroom is like.

While the lecture is considered low-impact engagement, strategically placed rhetorical questions trigger students' attention momentarily as they continue to record notes for later personal internalization. Rhetorical questions can be intentionally planned and spotted throughout the lecture notes for optimum effect in sparking students' thoughts. Skillful lecturers seem to know when to signal students' attention in this otherwise one-way broadcast model.

## Model #1

(Source: Perhaps Professor Kingsfield, from *The Paper Chase*)

Lecture/Rhetorical Questioning: Teacher Talk

## PRESCRIPTION

Use with large groups and/or lots of information; punctuate the teacher talk with rhetorical questions throughout.

## DESCRIPTION

As part of a required pre-med course on the ethics of technology, 200 university students attend an hour lecture twice a week.

■ ■ ■

| Notes | Vignette |
|---|---|
| Lecture Input (or Teacher Talk) | *With the breakthroughs in medical technology, the options for life support systems are increasing at a rapid rate.* |
| Rhetorical Question | *How do you think that affects us?* |
| Teacher | [Pauses for moment then continues lecture] |
| Lecture Input (or Teacher Talk) | *It seems quite straight forward to make a technical decision. But one must consider all the implications of that decision.* |
| Rhetorical Question | *Haven't we all faced a dilemma such as this?* |
| Teacher | [Pauses for moment then continues lecture] |

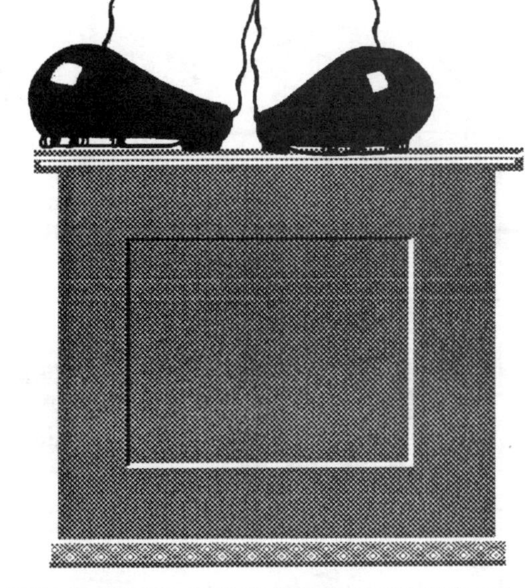

# LESSON PLANNER

## Think Abouts . . .

What is an appropriate use? What is an inappropriate use? When might I *overlook* this strategy? Why?

Can I "steal" the idea illustrated in the vignette? Do I want to *duplicate* it?

Is there an existing lesson I can redesign to *replicate* this strategy?

How can I fold this into a lesson I've planned? Does it *integrate* or connect with something I already do?

How can I bridge this into several areas? Where else can I *map* this for additional practice and transfer?

What idea is percolating? Can I *innovate* using some key aspect of this strategy?

## My Lesson Idea

Topic or Unit:__________________________

_______________________________________

My purpose for this lesson:

_______________________________________

_______________________________________

_______________________________________

_______________________________________

My idea . . . in a nutshell:

_______________________________________

_______________________________________

_______________________________________

_______________________________________

_______________________________________

_______________________________________

_______________________________________

_______________________________________

_______________________________________

Why this strategy seems right:

_______________________________________

_______________________________________

_______________________________________

_______________________________________

_______________________________________

_______________________________________

Other thoughts:

_______________________________________

_______________________________________

_______________________________________

_______________________________________

# DOUBLE-ENTRY JOURNAL: PROCESSING

| Description of the Lesson | Reflections on the Lesson |
| --- | --- |
| **What I did before the lesson:** | **Thoughts, ideas, connections I'm making . . .** |
| **What I did during the lesson:** | |
| **What I did following the lesson:** | |

*There are three great questions which in life we have over and over again to answer: Is it right or wrong? Is it true or false? Is it beautiful or ugly? Our education ought to help us to answer these questions.*—John Lubbock

# SIGNALS/DIRECT QUESTIONING: SURVEYING

Knowing that students can attend to a lecture for approximately seven minutes, the teacher surveys with a total group response or samples with a direct question to see how students are understanding the information.

The use of physical responses, such as raised hands and thumbs up, to signal opinions or to take a quick barometric reading of an audience is a proven strategy of the seasoned teacher. The skilled practitioner spontaneously calls for raised hands or stand-and-be-counted action to make a point or to accentuate differences in positions. Typically, openers such as "If you agree...." "Raise your hand if you...." or "Would you rather . . .?" lead this physical response strategy in which all students are expected to participate. Even though accountability for involvement is often not tailored into these interactions, for quick overviews this strategy can be quite effective.

The experienced teacher also asks learners pointed questions to elicit in-depth responses and sample student responsibility. As a student grapples with the direct question and searches for elaborative examples to support the ideas, other students are engaged vicariously in the student-teacher interchange. However, since direct questions do not necessarily *directly* involve all students, the experienced teacher keeps these interchanges short and appropriately uses them with signaling questions that involve the entire group.

**Model #2**

(Source: Hunter)

## PRESCRIPTION

Use to make lectures slightly interactive—á la interactive video model in which students are hooked momentarily—with a total group physical response or one student's in-depth answer.



## DESCRIPTION

As the high school biology teacher punctuates his DNA lecture with signaling questions, he deliberately weaves direct questions into the lecture for occasional in-depth student responses.

■ ■ ■

| Notes | Vignette |
|---|---|
| Signaling Question | *How many agree? Raise your hands.* |
| Teacher | [Pauses and looks for responses] |
| Students | [Raise hands] |
| Signaling Question | *How many disagree?* |
| Teacher | [Pauses and looks for responses] |
| Students | [Raise hands] |
| Teacher | [Continues lecture] |
| Direct Question | *David, tell us why you agree with the text. You believe the assumptions are true.* |
| Student | *Well, I'm not sure, but I was connecting this idea to . . . .* |

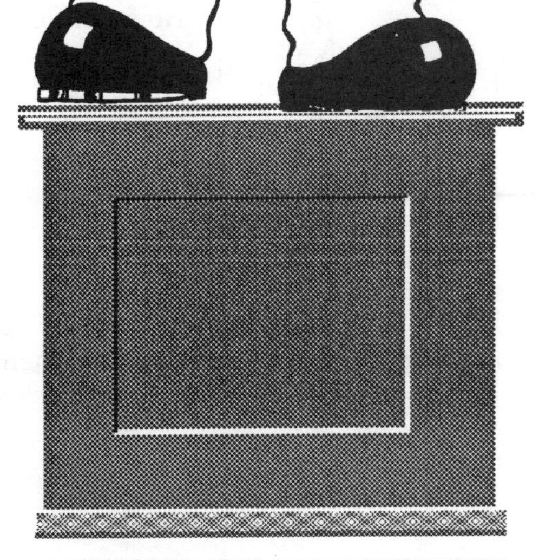

# LESSON PLANNER

## Think Abouts . . .

What is an appropriate use? What is an inappropriate use? When might I *overlook* this strategy? Why?

Can I "steal" the idea illustrated in the vignette? Do I want to *duplicate* it?

Is there an existing lesson I can redesign to *replicate* this strategy?

How can I fold this into a lesson I've planned? Does it *integrate* or connect with something I already do?

How can I bridge this into several areas? Where else can I *map* this for additional practice and transfer?

What idea is percolating? Can I *innovate* using some key aspect of this strategy?

## My Lesson Idea

Topic or Unit:____________________

______________________________

My purpose for this lesson:

______________________________

______________________________

______________________________

______________________________

My idea . . . in a nutshell:

______________________________

______________________________

______________________________

______________________________

______________________________

______________________________

______________________________

______________________________

______________________________

Why this strategy seems right:

______________________________

______________________________

______________________________

______________________________

______________________________

______________________________

Other thoughts:

______________________________

______________________________

______________________________

______________________________

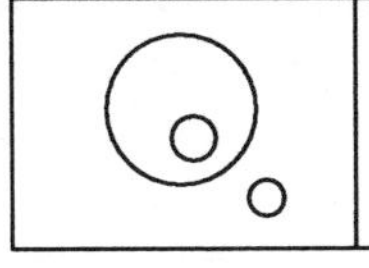



## DOUBLE-ENTRY JOURNAL: PROCESSING

| Description of the Lesson | Reflections on the Lesson |
|---|---|
| What I did before the lesson: | Thoughts, ideas, connections I'm making . . . |
| What I did during the lesson: | |
| What I did following the lesson: | |

*Learn to reason forward and backward on both sides of a question.*—Thomas Blandi

# TURN TO YOUR PARTNER AND . . . (TTYPA)

TTYPA, or Turn To Your Partner And . . ., is a natural reflex for teachers moving toward more interactive classrooms. Instead of imagining a classroom of passive students and docile thinkers working in isolation ("Keep your eyes on your own work!"), the new school "lecture" pictures students talking to each other as they explore personal connections to the topic under discussion.

Interestingly, merely by articulating ideas to each other, students seem to enhance their memory and learning. Just as writing down one's goals lends power to the accomplishment of those goals, talking about ideas lends power to students' thinking and learning about those ideas.

With this TTYPA strategy, teachers make clear their high expectations for students' interaction. It is next to impossible to turn to your partner and . . . not say something. This simple strategy has a compelling ingredient in it. There is a built-in expectation for reciprocity. It's hard to drop out of a twosome when your partner is depending on you to complete the interaction. For this reason, TTYPA has an edge over the previously described interaction designs. TTYPA has the "sink or swim together" element that cooperative learning research supports. TTYPA, although less formal than many interactive models, engages students quickly and interdependently.

## Model #3

(Source: Weaver & Cotrell)

## PRESCRIPTION

Use to punctuate a lecture, a film or a reading to actively cue and engage student thinking.

## DESCRIPTION

In a lesson on thinking, the teacher has her eighth-grade students walk down memory lane to demonstrate the differences between cognitive and metacognitive thinking.

■ ■ ■

| Notes | Vignette |
|---|---|
| Lecture Input | *Metacognition is thinking about your thinking. Let me demonstrate.* |
| TTYPA | *Turn to your partner and recite a piece you know by memory. Then, switch roles with your partner.* |
| Student A | *Four score and seven years ago . . .* |
| Student B | *We the people of the United States . . .* |
| Lecturer | *That's called cognition. Now, TTYPA tell how you learned that piece so well that you could say it today.* |
| Student A | *I learned by repeating . . .* |
| Student B | *By creating a song . . .* |
| Lecturer | *Thinking about how you learned is called metacognition.* |

## LESSON PLANNER

### Think Abouts . . .

What is an appropriate use? What is an inappropriate use? When might I *overlook* this strategy? Why?

Can I "steal" the idea illustrated in the vignette? Do I want to *duplicate* it?

Is there an existing lesson I can redesign to *replicate* this strategy?

How can I fold this into a lesson I've planned? Does it *integrate* or connect with something I already do?

How can I bridge this into several areas? Where else can I *map* this for additional practice and transfer?

What idea is percolating? Can I *innovate* using some key aspect of this strategy?

### My Lesson Idea

Topic or Unit:______________________________

______________________________

My purpose for this lesson:

______________________________

______________________________

______________________________

______________________________

My idea . . . in a nutshell:

______________________________

______________________________

______________________________

______________________________

______________________________

______________________________

______________________________

______________________________

______________________________

Why this strategy seems right:

______________________________

______________________________

______________________________

______________________________

______________________________

______________________________

Other thoughts:

______________________________

______________________________

______________________________

______________________________

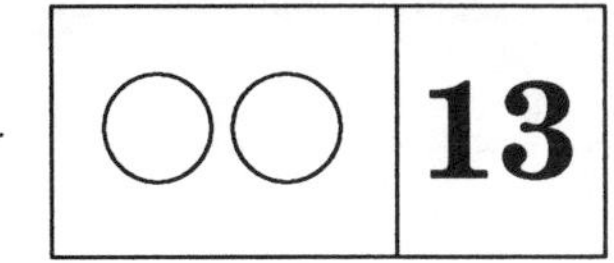


## DOUBLE-ENTRY JOURNAL: PROCESSING

| Description of the Lesson | Reflections on the Lesson |
| --- | --- |
| **What I did before the lesson:** | **Thoughts, ideas, connections I'm making . . .** |
| **What I did during the lesson:** | |
| **What I did following the lesson:** | |

*There's a mighty big difference between good, sound reasons and reasons that sound good.*—Burton Hillis

# PAIRED PARTNERS: THINK ALOUD

As described by Whimbey, the paired partners, think aloud design couples students in a tutorial model. One student becomes the problem solver and the other student becomes the monitor. The problem solver talks aloud throughout the task, giving a running monologue of thoughts, strategies, ideas and notions for solving the problem.

The monitor cues the "self-talk" of the problem solver with appropriate questions: What is your purpose? What are you expecting? Does that make sense? Why? What are you thinking? Did you skip a step?

The focus of this strategy is to help students make their thinking visible so they can track their patterns for thinking. By making their thinking evident, students can spot their faulty reasoning and strategies for thinking.

Although this design requires intense, guided practice for effective partner work, its strength should not be overlooked. The think aloud design provides a human mirror-reflection of students' thinking and can be adapted across subject matter. Used over time with the same partners, this design allows students to become familiar enough to unveil each other's patterns for thinking. By practicing and perfecting the metacognitive tracking of a partner, students reap the long-term benefits of becoming skilled in and reflective about their approaches to problem solving.

**Model #4**

(Source: Bloom; Whimbey)

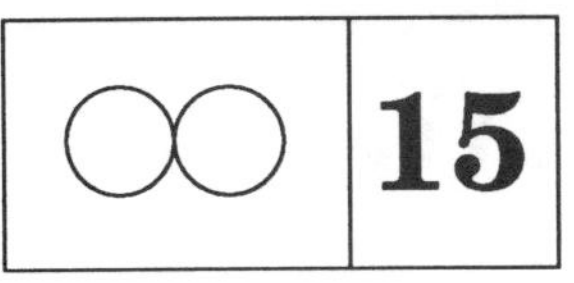

## PRESCRIPTION

Use over time to develop metacognitive, think-aloud tracking of students' behaviors in problem-solving or decision-making interactions.

## DESCRIPTION

During a sixth-grade math lesson, one partner thinks aloud while solving a problem. The monitor cues the thinking with questions.

■ ■ ■

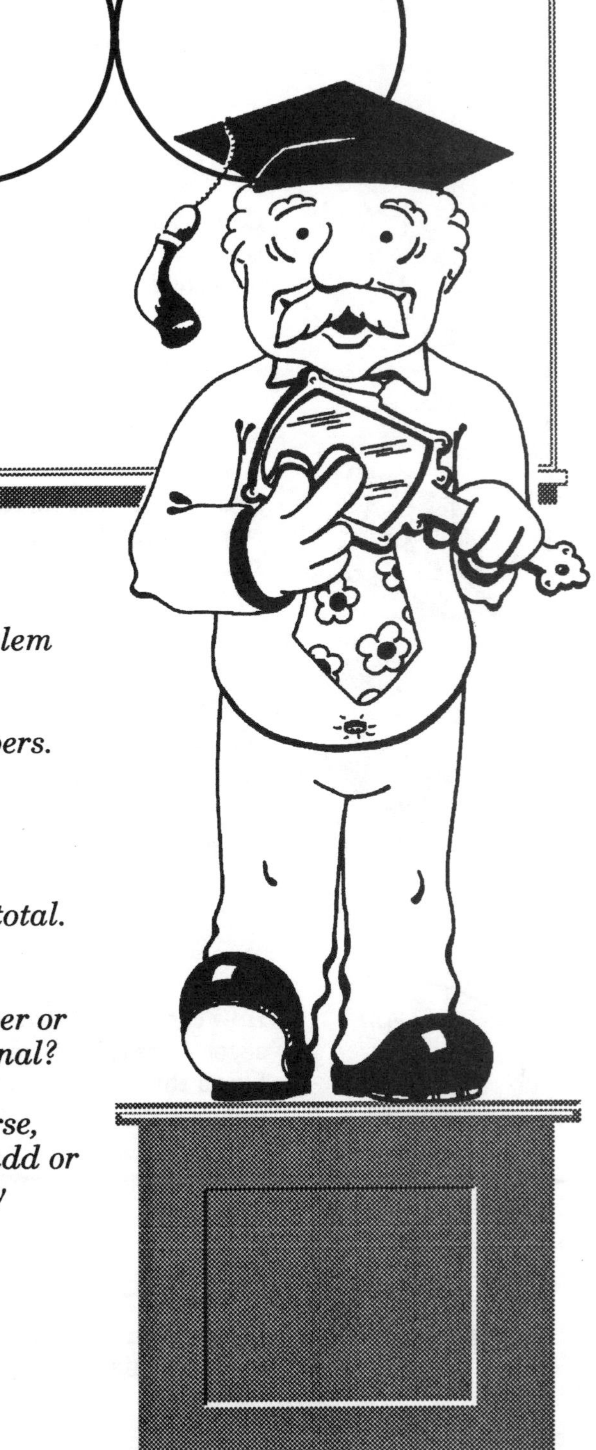


| Notes | Vignette |
|---|---|
| Think Aloud | *In partners, solve this story problem using the think aloud strategy.* |
| Problem solver thinks aloud. | *I'm going to add these two numbers. Then, I'll . . . .* |
| Monitor asks questions. | *Why are you doing that?* |
| Problem solver elaborates upon thought. | *Because the question calls for a total.* |
| Monitor asks questions. | *Are you expecting a larger number or a smaller number than the original?* |
| Problem solver elaborates upon the thought and catches another for a new strategy. | *I'm thinking the number, of course, will be larger. Therefore, I will add or multiply. Hmm, could I multiply here?* |
| Monitor notes one of the problem solver's thinking patterns. | *Last time you started with . . . .* |

# LESSON PLANNER

## Think Abouts . . .

What is an appropriate use? What is an inappropriate use? When might I *overlook* this strategy? Why?

Can I "steal" the idea illustrated in the vignette? Do I want to *duplicate* it?

Is there an existing lesson I can redesign to *replicate* this strategy?

How can I fold this into a lesson I've planned? Does it *integrate* or connect with something I already do?

How can I bridge this into several areas? Where else can I *map* this for additional practice and transfer?

What idea is percolating? Can I *innovate* using some key aspect of this strategy?

## My Lesson Idea

Topic or Unit:______________________________

____________________________________________

My purpose for this lesson:

____________________________________________

____________________________________________

____________________________________________

____________________________________________

My idea . . . in a nutshell:

____________________________________________

____________________________________________

____________________________________________

____________________________________________

____________________________________________

____________________________________________

____________________________________________

____________________________________________

____________________________________________

Why this strategy seems right:

____________________________________________

____________________________________________

____________________________________________

____________________________________________

____________________________________________

____________________________________________

Other thoughts:

____________________________________________

____________________________________________

____________________________________________

____________________________________________

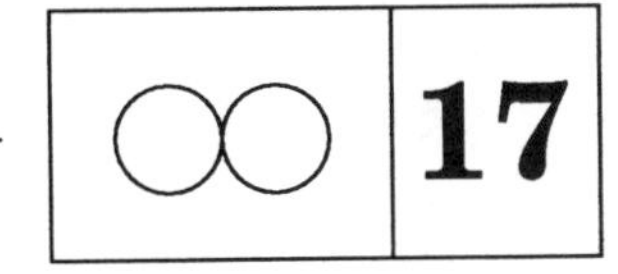


## DOUBLE-ENTRY JOURNAL: PROCESSING

| Description of the Lesson | Reflections on the Lesson |
|---|---|
| **What I did before the lesson:** | **Thoughts, ideas, connections I'm making . . .** |
| **What I did during the lesson:** | |
| **What I did following the lesson:** | |

*Personally I'm always ready to learn, although I do not always like being taught.*—Winston Churchill

# DYADS: THINK/PAIR/SHARE

Lyman's think/pair/share strategy illustrates the skilled use of a theory-embedded tool. In the think/pair/share design of cooperative interaction a teacher's question is deliberately followed by 3 to 10 seconds of silence, called "wait time" by its original researcher Mary Budd Rowe.

After giving students sufficient wait time to think through a question and make some personal connections, the teacher instructs the pairs to share their thinking with each other.

Think ➔ Pair ➔ Share

As students begin to share their ideas, each partner benefits from the other's perspectives. As in other interaction models, students' thinking is supported by the articulation of an idea. It's one thing to think about an idea or opinion inside one's own head; it's quite another thing to try to explain that thinking to someone else.

In the sharing, partners retrace their words, search for telling examples and clarify the fuzziness in their own thinking. The teacher may even ask the partners to compromise or synthesize their ideas into one idea. By using both wait time and "talk time," this structured interaction offers a myriad of beneficial opportunities in all classrooms.

**Model #5**

**(Source: Lyman & McTighe)**

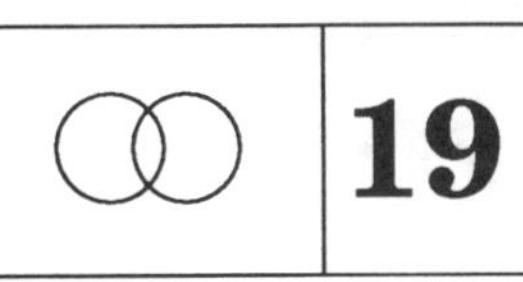


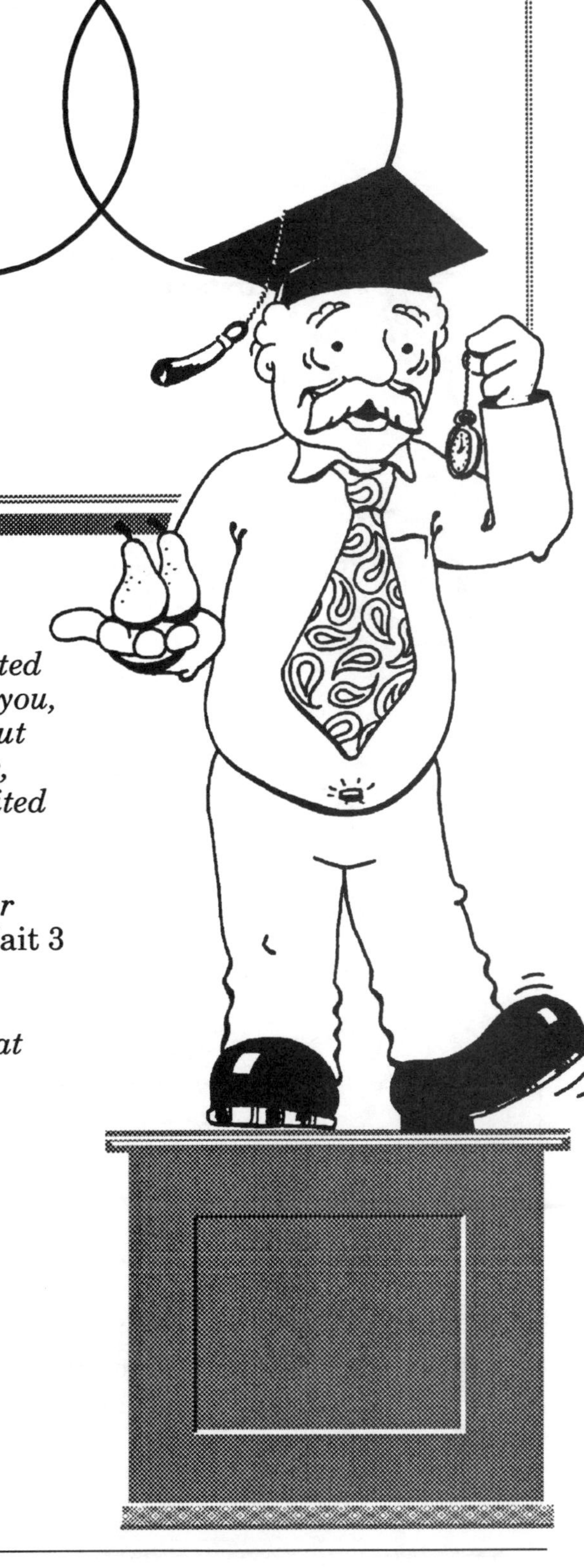


## PRESCRIPTION

Use when formal wait time is needed for making connections, reaching consensus or prompting thoughtful articulation.

## DESCRIPTION

The non-listening game is used to teach third-graders the social skill of active listening. By exaggerating the *opposite* of a desired classroom behavior, students are focused on the desired behavior.

■ ■ ■

| Notes | Vignette |
|---|---|
| Activity Input | *You and your partner just completed the non-listening game. As one of you, the "speaker," spoke in length about something of personal importance, your partner, the "listener," exhibited non-listening behaviors.* |
| Think (alone) | *Think about the things the listener did that signaled* no *listening.* [Wait 3 to 10 seconds] |
| Pair/Share | *Now, share with your partner what you saw and how you felt.* |
| Listener | *I looked away.* |
| Speaker | *You interrupted me.* |
| Listener | *I felt bad because I knew I wasn't paying attention. It was rude.* |
| Speaker | *I wanted to quit talking to you.* |

## LESSON PLANNER

### Think Abouts . . .

What is an appropriate use? What is an inappropriate use? When might I *overlook* this strategy? Why?

Can I "steal" the idea illustrated in the vignette? Do I want to *duplicate* it?

Is there an existing lesson I can redesign to *replicate* this strategy?

How can I fold this into a lesson I've planned? Does it *integrate* or connect with something I already do?

How can I bridge this into several areas? Where else can I *map* this for additional practice and transfer?

What idea is percolating? Can I *innovate* using some key aspect of this strategy?

### My Lesson Idea

Topic or Unit:____________________

______________________________

My purpose for this lesson:

______________________________

______________________________

______________________________

______________________________

My idea . . . in a nutshell:

______________________________

______________________________

______________________________

______________________________

______________________________

______________________________

______________________________

______________________________

______________________________

Why this strategy seems right:

______________________________

______________________________

______________________________

______________________________

______________________________

______________________________

Other thoughts:

______________________________

______________________________

______________________________

______________________________

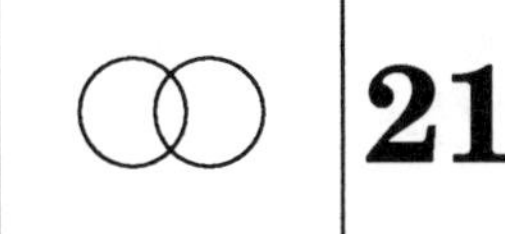


## DOUBLE-ENTRY JOURNAL: PROCESSING

| Description of the Lesson | Reflections on the Lesson |
|---|---|
| **What I did before the lesson:** | **Thoughts, ideas, connections I'm making . . .** |
| **What I did during the lesson:** | |
| **What I did following the lesson:** | |

*It requires a very unusual mind to make an analysis of the obvious.*—Alfred North Whitehead

# TRIADS: OBSERVER FEEDBACK

The term triads designates the interactive design that embraces standard partner work with the extension of an observer. In particular situations it is advantageous to assign a partner task and simultaneously designate a third group member to observe the partner interaction and to provide immediate, verifiable feedback.

The observer's role lends an added dimension to the partners' interaction. While partners may practice the desired behavior or perform the assigned task, it is often difficult for them to track their own progress. To master a cognitive behavior requires conscious effort on the part of the novice learner and to track one's progress requires further conscious effort. Therefore, to monitor the performance, one must stand outside the actual act to look in, as it were, on the action. In this triad design, the observer is apart from the interaction.

Stepping out of the situation to peer in is called metacognition—or "beyond the cognitive." The assigned observer in this design is already outside the action. Having the observer look in on the interaction, record observable data and give the pair feedback is a viable cooperative model that affords valuable learning opportunities.

It is important to note that the observer in this case is separate from the partner interaction and not a participating member as in other triad models. The observer is out of the interaction, looking in to give objective and accurate feedback.

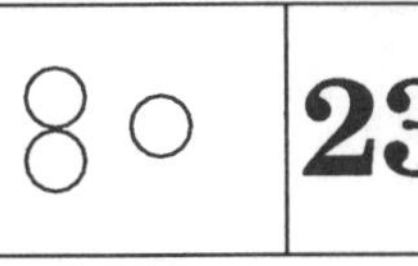


Triads: Observer Feedback

## PRESCRIPTION

Use when partner interactions can be elaborated by objective observer feedback—when student pairs may be so involved in the interaction that an outside observer is needed.

## DESCRIPTION

To teach the use of higher-order questions, the teacher introduces eleventh-grade students to fat and skinny questions and then asks the students to practice them in trios.

■ ■ ■

| Notes | Vignette |
|---|---|
| Observer | *I will be noting FAT and Skinny questions. FAT questions elicit elaborated answers with examples and details. Skinny questions get yes, no, maybe and other one-word answers.* |
| Interviewer | *How do you compare and contrast democracy to socialism?* |
| Observer | [Records FAT question] |
| Interviewee | *Similarities might include ___ while differences include ___.* |
| Interviewer | *Which do you prefer?* |
| Observer | [Records Skinny question] |
| Interviewee | *The former!* |
| Interviewer | *Imagine justifying your choice. What might you say?* |
| Observer | [Records FAT question] |
| Observer | *I recorded ___ FAT questions and ___ Skinny questions.* |

| FAT | Skinny |
|---|---|
| II | 𝍸 |

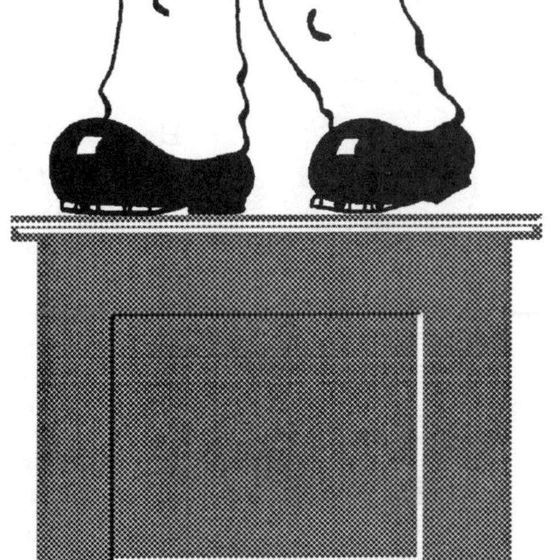

## LESSON PLANNER

### Think Abouts . . .

What is an appropriate use? What is an inappropriate use? When might I *overlook* this strategy? Why?

Can I "steal" the idea illustrated in the vignette? Do I want to *duplicate* it?

Is there an existing lesson I can redesign to *replicate* this strategy?

How can I fold this into a lesson I've planned? Does it *integrate* or connect with something I already do?

How can I bridge this into several areas? Where else can I *map* this for additional practice and transfer?

What idea is percolating? Can I *innovate* using some key aspect of this strategy?

### My Lesson Idea

Topic or Unit:____________________________

________________________________________

My purpose for this lesson:

________________________________________

________________________________________

________________________________________

________________________________________

My idea . . . in a nutshell:

________________________________________

________________________________________

________________________________________

________________________________________

________________________________________

________________________________________

________________________________________

________________________________________

________________________________________

Why this strategy seems right:

________________________________________

________________________________________

________________________________________

________________________________________

________________________________________

________________________________________

Other thoughts:

________________________________________

________________________________________

________________________________________

________________________________________

## DOUBLE-ENTRY JOURNAL: PROCESSING

| Description of the Lesson | Reflections on the Lesson |
| --- | --- |
| What I did before the lesson: | Thoughts, ideas, connections I'm making . . . |
| What I did during the lesson: | |
| What I did following the lesson: | |

*Whenever two people meet there are really six people present. There is each man as he sees himself, each man as the other person sees him, and each man as he really is.*—William James

# TELL/RETELL: 2-4-8

The 2-4-8 model gives rigorous attention to both expressive skills (speaking) and receptive (listening) skills.

In the 2-4-8 model, students begin by talking in pairs. A *tells* a story to B, and B in turn *tells* a story to A.

(A)
(B)

Now, A and B join another pair of partners, C and D, for whom they each must *retell* the *other's* story. With the stories freshly told and with the added motivation of the original "teller" scrutinizing the "retelling," A *retells* B's story to C and D. Then B *retells* A's story to C and D. In turn, C *retells* D's story and D *retells* C's story.

(A)(C)
(B)(D)

You guessed it. Now, A, B, C and D move to a group of eight, and no one may *retell* a story he/she has already *told* or *retold*. Each member of the eight relates a third story.

Following the eight stories (which are now quite succinct), group members try to recall all eight interactions. This is truly a test of active listening. Once the groups begin, they may rely on artifacts, student work used in the tellings and retellings, as memory joggers.

**Model #7**

**(Source: Fogarty & Bellanca)**

Tell/Retell: 2-4-8

## PRESCRIPTION

Use to structure active listening in a partner sharing or for quickly gathering lots of ideas.

## DESCRIPTION

In a typical primary classroom, show and tell is structured carefully for developing students' speaking and listening skills.

■ ■ ■

### Notes

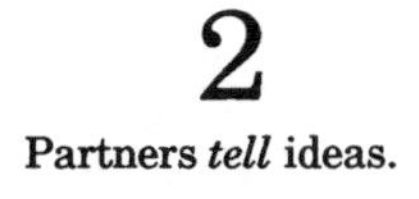

2

Partners *tell* ideas.

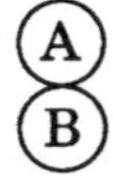

4

A *retells* B's. B *retells* A's. C *retells* D's. D *retells* C's.

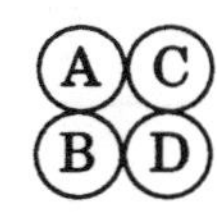

8

Each *retells* new story.

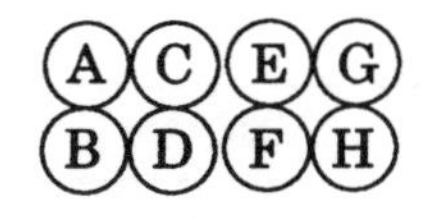

### Vignette

A: *This is my skin from a snake. I found it on the hiking path. The snake wiggled out of it while getting a suntan.*
B: *I bought my favorite Transformer®. My dad couldn't figure it out. I had to help him. It's pretty tricky.*

A: *"B" brought the Transformer® that his dad couldn't figure out.*
B: *"A" found a snake's skin while hiking.*
C: *"D" brought photographs of his birthday party at the pizza place.*
D: *"C" forgot her show and tell but she told me about her ride in the row boat.*

A: *"C" forgot hers but she rode in a boat.*
B: *"D" has pictures of the pizza place.*
C: *"B" can transform his Transformer®.*
D: *"A" has the skin of a snake.*
E: *"G" played the harmonica.*
F: *"H" wore her sister's hair ribbons.*
G: *"F" has colored marbles.*
H: *"E" brought his new book.*

# LESSON PLANNER

## Think Abouts . . .

What is an appropriate use? What is an inappropriate use? When might I *overlook* this strategy? Why?

Can I "steal" the idea illustrated in the vignette? Do I want to *duplicate* it?

Is there an existing lesson I can redesign to *replicate* this strategy?

How can I fold this into a lesson I've planned? Does it *integrate* or connect with something I already do?

How can I bridge this into several areas? Where else can I *map* this for additional practice and transfer?

What idea is percolating? Can I *innovate* using some key aspect of this strategy?

## My Lesson Idea

Topic or Unit:____________________________

________________________________________

My purpose for this lesson:

________________________________________

________________________________________

________________________________________

________________________________________

My idea . . . in a nutshell:

________________________________________

________________________________________

________________________________________

________________________________________

________________________________________

________________________________________

________________________________________

________________________________________

________________________________________

Why this strategy seems right:

________________________________________

________________________________________

________________________________________

________________________________________

________________________________________

________________________________________

Other thoughts:

________________________________________

________________________________________

________________________________________

________________________________________

## DOUBLE-ENTRY JOURNAL: PROCESSING

| Description of the Lesson | Reflections on the Lesson |
| --- | --- |
| **What I did before the lesson:** | **Thoughts, ideas, connections I'm making . . .** |
| **What I did during the lesson:** | |
| **What I did following the lesson:** | |

*Man is a social animal.*— Spinoza

# COOPERATIVE LEARNING: GROUPS

Cooperative learning groups, as promoted by the Johnsons, embrace five key elements: positive interdependence, individual accountability, group processing, social skills and face-to-face interaction. Typically, three to five students are placed in heterogeneous groups with an academic task and a specific social skill targeted.

Positive interdependence, a "sink or swim together" (Johnsons) attitude, is tailored into the group work so that the success of each member depends on the success of the group. This can be achieved by accepting only one product from the group. Assigned roles can provide individual accountability in a setting that promotes head-to-head interaction.

To complete the critical elements of cooperative learning, group members talk about their progress with the targeted social skill. This metacognitive "talking about" the social behavior facilitates transfer of the social skill into other settings.

Slavin and Kagan complement on this conceptual model of the Johnsons'. Slavin's curriculum packages engage students in team tasks that carry high motivation and high rewards. Kagan develops a rich repertoire of structures (strategies) that the skillful teacher can slot immediately into the classroom curriculum.

In essence, cooperative learning, or "groups," is the formal model in which students are encouraged to reach out to others in structured small-group activities.

## Model #8

(Source: Johnson & Johnson; Kagan; Slavin)

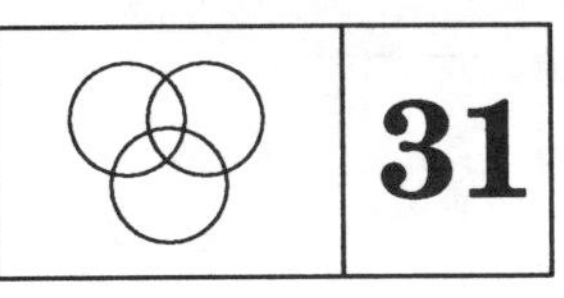

## PRESCRIPTION

Use to engage students in the learning process—particularly with activities that involve them intensely in the learning.

## DESCRIPTION

Cooperative groups are used in a seventh-grade Directed Reading Thinking Activity (DRTA) to predict and justify what students think about a story.

■ ■ ■

| Notes | Vignette |
|---|---|
| Checker checks for understanding. | *Does everyone understand? We will use BET.* |
| (Teacher monitors.) | **B**ase on facts<br>**E**xpress possibilities<br>**T**ender a bet on what we think will happen next in "The Dinner Party." |
| Encourager encourages responses in turn.<br>(Teacher monitors.) | *I think it's a murder mystery because of the title.* |
| Checker gives response. | *I think it's about cannibals. There will be a twist.* |
| Recorder gives response. | *Maybe it's about animals having a tea party. This is from school, you know.* |
| Encourager gathers group consensus. | *Let's write down the cannibal idea because it's so different. What do the rest of you think?* |
| Recorder | [Writes down group answer] |

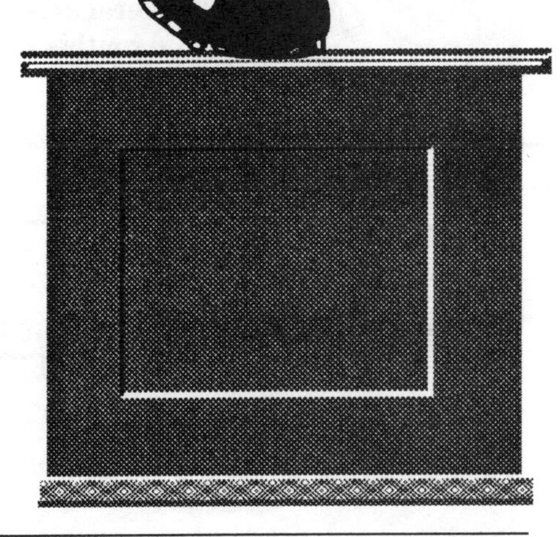

# LESSON PLANNER

## Think Abouts . . .

What is an appropriate use? What is an inappropriate use? When might I *overlook* this strategy? Why?

Can I "steal" the idea illustrated in the vignette? Do I want to *duplicate* it?

Is there an existing lesson I can redesign to *replicate* this strategy?

How can I fold this into a lesson I've planned? Does it *integrate* or connect with something I already do?

How can I bridge this into several areas? Where else can I *map* this for additional practice and transfer?

What idea is percolating? Can I *innovate* using some key aspect of this strategy?

## My Lesson Idea

Topic or Unit: ________________________________

________________________________________

My purpose for this lesson:

________________________________________

________________________________________

________________________________________

________________________________________

My idea . . . in a nutshell:

________________________________________

________________________________________

________________________________________

________________________________________

________________________________________

________________________________________

________________________________________

________________________________________

________________________________________

Why this strategy seems right:

________________________________________

________________________________________

________________________________________

________________________________________

________________________________________

________________________________________

Other thoughts:

________________________________________

________________________________________

________________________________________

________________________________________

# DOUBLE-ENTRY JOURNAL: PROCESSING

## Description of the Lesson

**What I did before the lesson:**

**What I did during the lesson:**

**What I did following the lesson:**

## Reflections on the Lesson

**Thoughts, ideas, connections I'm making . . .**

*The best things and best people rise out of their separateness; I'm against a homogenized society because I want the cream to rise.*—Robert Frost

# TRAVELING CLUSTERS: PEOPLE SEARCH

A proven ice-breaker, the people search, invites participants to move about the room and talk with each other while gathering answers to questions. Cued with a list of statements beginning with, "Find someone who . . .," participants make informal clusters of two, three or four students as they sample other people's ideas and gather signatures. The focus of the search can be strictly on socializing and getting to know one another, or the questions can engage students in thoughtful deliberations about an academic topic. This design can be used as a pre-learning activity to stir up students' prior knowledge or as a review before a test.

The people search is not only an invitation to meet others, but an unmistakable message about the climate of the classroom. The people search signals to students that it's OK to talk, move about the room and even to disagree and debate ideas. It suggests that everyone is a resource in the classroom, not just the teacher.

By structuring "traveling clusters," students are given some choice in selecting their "partners." At the same time, they are also encouraged to meet different people. In motivating students to seek out new or unknown classmates, the people search provides golden opportunities for teachers to talk to students about how to meet new people or how to enter into new groups. The skillful teacher gets lots of mileage out of this simple strategy.

## Model #9

(Source: Workshop Leaders)

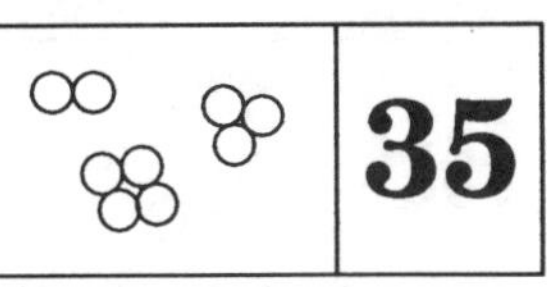


Traveling Clusters: People Search

## PRESCRIPTION

Use as an ice-breaker, as a pre-learning strategy to activate prior knowledge, or as a review prior to a test.

## DESCRIPTION

To stir up prior knowledge for a high school lesson about thinking skills, the people search cue sheet starts the student interaction.

■ ■ ■

| **Notes** | **Vignette** |
|---|---|
| People Search | *Everyone move about the room and search for people you can talk with about the activities listed on your sheet.* |

> FIND SOMEONE WHO . . .
> 1. Can classify friends. ______________ (signature)
> 2. Can name problem-solving steps. ______________ (signature)
> 3. Can . . .
> 4. Can . . .

| | |
|---|---|
| Student A | *I think I can classify friends into four groups.* |
| Student B | *Great. Go ahead.* |
| Student A | *The good, the bad, the ugly and best friend.* |
| Student B | *Super. Maybe, I can help you with the steps to problem solving. First, decide on the real problem....* |
| Student A | *Thanks. Talk to you later.* |
| Teacher | *Continue to move to newly forming clusters of two, three or four students.* |

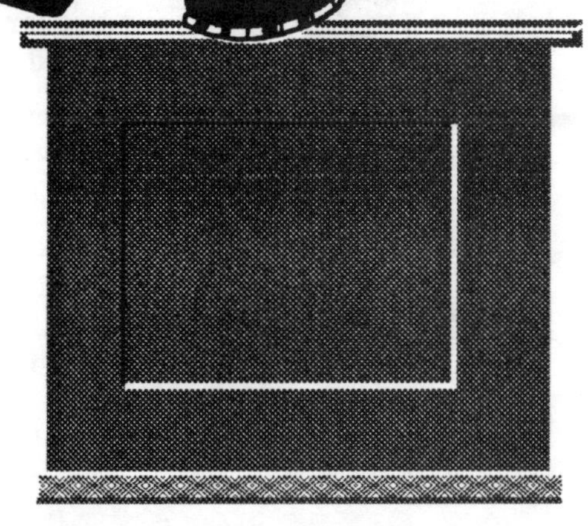

# LESSON PLANNER

## Think Abouts . . .

What is an appropriate use? What is an inappropriate use? When might I *overlook* this strategy? Why?

Can I "steal" the idea illustrated in the vignette? Do I want to *duplicate* it?

Is there an existing lesson I can redesign to *replicate* this strategy?

How can I fold this into a lesson I've planned? Does it *integrate* or connect with something I already do?

How can I bridge this into several areas? Where else can I *map* this for additional practice and transfer?

What idea is percolating? Can I *innovate* using some key aspect of this strategy?

## My Lesson Idea

Topic or Unit: ____________________

____________________

My purpose for this lesson:

____________________
____________________
____________________
____________________

My idea . . . in a nutshell:

____________________
____________________
____________________
____________________
____________________
____________________
____________________
____________________
____________________

Why this strategy seems right:

____________________
____________________
____________________
____________________
____________________
____________________

Other thoughts:

____________________
____________________
____________________
____________________

## DOUBLE-ENTRY JOURNAL: PROCESSING

### Description of the Lesson

**What I did before the lesson:**

**What I did during the lesson:**

**What I did following the lesson:**

### Reflections on the Lesson

**Thoughts, ideas, connections I'm making . . .**

*Every individual has a place to fill in the world and is important in some respect whether he chooses to be so or not.*

—Nathaniel Hawthorne

# FORCED RESPONSE: WRAPAROUND

The use of the forced response strategy, sometimes called a wraparound, whip or snake, sets up the expectation that as the student responses proceed around the room, each person will contribute—thus the strategy name, forced response. By structuring this response-in-turn or round-robin model, students are automatically allotted a "spot and a slot" to share their comments.

The wraparound may be cued initially as an individual journal entry, giving students a moment to reflect and refine their thoughts. After completing the lead-in statement in writing, students stand to respond in the wraparound. As the responses snake around the room, the concept or idea takes on new dimensions through students' unique connections.

In reality, the forced response is not *really* forced since students are given an escape valve. Students can opt at any time to say, "I pass." Although most students take the challenge and respond in turn as expected, it is important to discuss this option and how it's properly used.

This wraparound design efficiently and effectively monitors individuals' reactions to a learning situation. It is especially useful for gathering quick response from each student to help anchor a concept or idea. Students are often surprised by the richness of the answers.

**Model #10**

(Source: Howe & Howe)

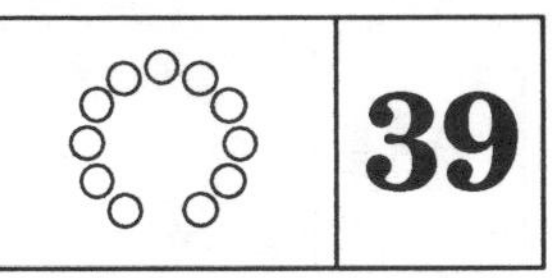


Forced Response: Wraparound

## PRESCRIPTION

Use over time throughout lessons to get quick responses and to set expectations for each student to respond.

## DESCRIPTION

At the close of a lesson, fifth-grade students are asked to compare thinking to an animal. After jotting down some ideas, a verbal wraparound is used to share the ideas and demonstrate the use of analogies.

■ ■ ■

| Notes | Vignette |
|---|---|
| Forced Response: Wraparound | *Everyone take a minute to jot down what thinking is like. When you are done, stand up. We will wrap around the room to hear the responses once everyone is standing.* |
| Teacher | [Signals first person to begin] |
| Response of student A | *Thinking is like a frog because it hops around in your mind.* |
| Teacher | [Signals next student] |
| Student B | *Thinking is like an elephant because it's heavy on your mind.* |
| Teacher | [Nods] |
| Student C | *Thinking is like a horse because both can throw you.* |
| Student D | *Thinking is like the cat family because it helps to be in a group.* |
| Student E | *Thinking is like a monkey because you can fool around with both.* |
| Student F | *Thinking is like a chicken because both can lay an egg!* |

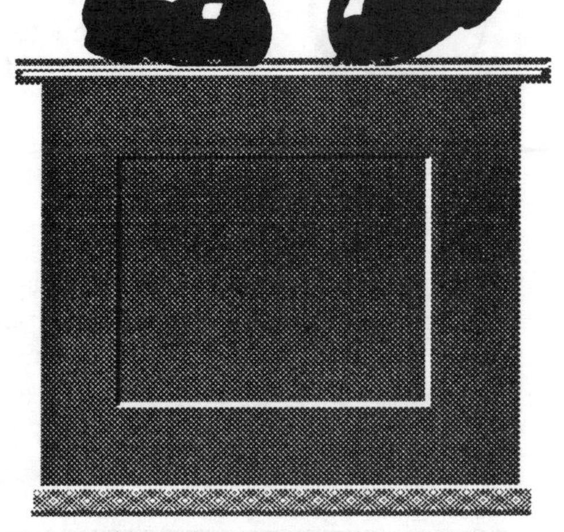

# LESSON PLANNER

## Think Abouts . . .

What is an appropriate use? What is an inappropriate use? When might I *overlook* this strategy? Why?

Can I "steal" the idea illustrated in the vignette? Do I want to *duplicate* it?

Is there an existing lesson I can redesign to *replicate* this strategy?

How can I fold this into a lesson I've planned? Does it *integrate* or connect with something I already do?

How can I bridge this into several areas? Where else can I *map* this for additional practice and transfer?

What idea is percolating? Can I *innovate* using some key aspect of this strategy?

## My Lesson Idea

Topic or Unit:______________________

______________________

My purpose for this lesson:

______________________

______________________

______________________

______________________

My idea . . . in a nutshell:

______________________

______________________

______________________

______________________

______________________

______________________

______________________

______________________

______________________

Why this strategy seems right:

______________________

______________________

______________________

______________________

______________________

______________________

Other thoughts:

______________________

______________________

______________________

______________________

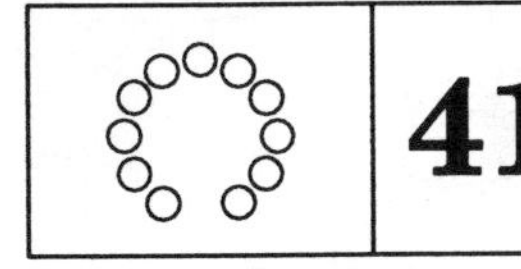

# DOUBLE-ENTRY JOURNAL: PROCESSING

| Description of the Lesson | Reflections on the Lesson |
| --- | --- |
| **What I did before the lesson:** | **Thoughts, ideas, connections I'm making . . .** |
| **What I did during the lesson:** | |
| **What I did following the lesson:** | |

*In all things that are purely social we can be as separate as the fingers, yet one as the hand in all things essential to mutual progress.*—Booker T. Washington

# TOTAL GROUP RESPONSE: HUMAN GRAPH

By requiring students to physically indicate their agreement/disagreement, preference or intensity of feelings on a given topic, the human graph quickly plots a total group response. The glory of this design is that it requires students to take a risk; they must take a public stand, advocate a position and support that position with details.

The teacher begins with a cuing statement or thought for which students literally take their stand on an imaginary or tape-drawn graph.

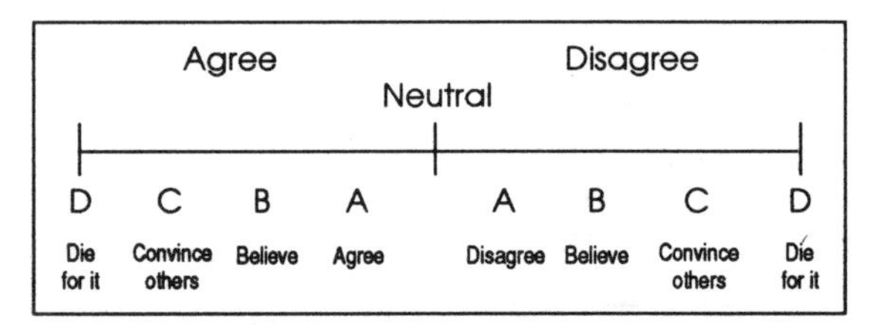


As the teacher samples students' reasoning, students are invited to rethink, modify and state their own opinions. Because this graph is a visible, living, breathing model, it can change instantly and repeatedly throughout the discussion. It reflects participants' changing opinions, invites negotiations and encourages empathic listening.

By verbalizing their positions, students prepare themselves for writing expositions. They also become metacognitively aware of their own decision-making behavior. For example: "I'm always in the middle. I can never make up my mind." "I didn't know how often I have such strong opinions." Students, will want to use the graph when discussions bubble up in the classroom . . . "Let's graph it!!!" And, vigorous conversations will continue as students drift out into the hall after class.

## Model #11

(Source: Johnson; Fogarty & Bellanca)

Total Group Response: Human Graph

## PRESCRIPTION

Use any time during a lesson to take a quick, but highly visible reading of the group members' feelings on an issue, idea or concept.

## DESCRIPTION

To introduce a ninth-grade unit on equity issues, the teacher structures an agree/disagree statement for sampling "public opinion."

■ ■ ■

| Notes | Vignette |
|---|---|
| Human Graph | *Indicate how strongly you agree or disagree with the following statement:* Women are stronger than men. |
| Students move on graph. | 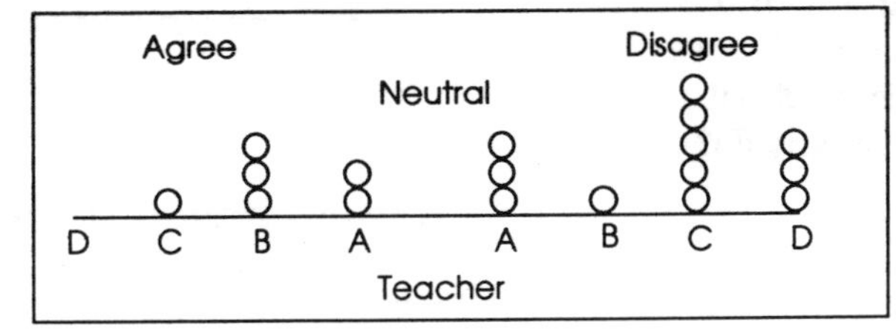  |
| Teacher samples students' reasoning. | *Why did you chose that spot?* |
| Student A | *Because I agree strongly. Think about the pioneer women and the hardships they had to overcome.* |
| Student B | *Oh yeah, I never thought of that. You're right. I'm going to move from this A (disagree) to that A (agree).* [Takes new position on graph] |

## LESSON PLANNER

### Think Abouts . . .

What is an appropriate use? What is an inappropriate use? When might I *overlook* this strategy? Why?

Can I "steal" the idea illustrated in the vignette? Do I want to *duplicate* it?

Is there an existing lesson I can redesign to *replicate* this strategy?

How can I fold this into a lesson I've planned? Does it *integrate* or connect with something I already do?

How can I bridge this into several areas? Where else can I *map* this for additional practice and transfer?

What idea is percolating? Can I *innovate* using some key aspect of this strategy?

### My Lesson Idea

Topic or Unit: ______________________________

______________________________

My purpose for this lesson:

______________________________

______________________________

______________________________

______________________________

My idea . . . in a nutshell:

______________________________

______________________________

______________________________

______________________________

______________________________

______________________________

______________________________

______________________________

______________________________

Why this strategy seems right:

______________________________

______________________________

______________________________

______________________________

______________________________

______________________________

Other thoughts:

______________________________

______________________________

______________________________

______________________________

## DOUBLE-ENTRY JOURNAL: PROCESSING

### Description of the Lesson

**What I did before the lesson:**

**What I did during the lesson:**

**What I did following the lesson:**

### Reflections on the Lesson

**Thoughts, ideas, connections I'm making . . .**

*No man is an island, entire of itself; every man is a piece of the continent, a part of the main.*—John Donne

# GROUP INVESTIGATION: JIGSAW

The cooperative interactive design is Sharans' group investigation model, which illustrates conceptually the ultimate jigsaw strategy. The jigsaw is an exquisite model of cooperation because the sink-or-swim-together element is inherent. However, caution must be taken so that the critical aspects of the jigsaw are practiced by all members.

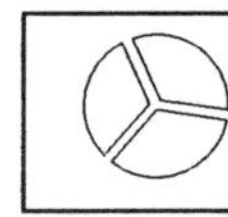

First, each member of a threesome selects or is assigned a piece of the group work. Second, members must sort and synthesize their pieces of the "puzzle" by gathering and organizing formation. Finally, the members must teach their

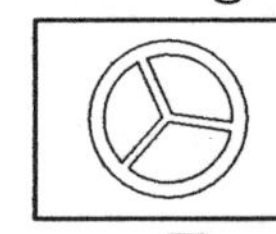

critical findings to the other group members so they *all* know *all* the pieces of the jigsaw as well as they know their own.

To perform the jigsaw effectively, students need explicit instructions in how to effectively share information so that others will learn it. Once mastered, however, the jigsaw is a key interactive design that leads to a number of variations on the theme.

For instance, teachers can design an "expert jigsaw" in which all groups get the same "puzzle pieces." Members meet with other groups' members who have the same piece (for example, the "ones" get together, the "twos," etc.). As the experts, they sort and synthesize the information together and then return to their groups to teach.

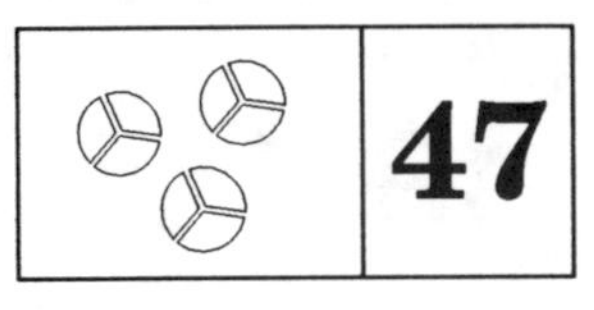

## PRESCRIPTION

Use when groups are socially sophisticated or to build individual responsibility within the team.

## DESCRIPTION

In a fourth-grade classroom, groups of three students are given different regions of the U.S. to investigate and research. Ultimately responsible for knowing all three regions, each group member teaches the others about a region.

■ ■ ■

| Notes | Vignette |
|---|---|
| Group Investigation: Jigsaw | *Have each member in your group research one of the following topics: the Eastern seaboard, the mid-section of the country, and the western portion of the United States.* |
| Student A | *I'm going to start in the library.* |
| Student B | *I need to define my area.* |
| Student C | *This is great. I love the west.* |
| Group Investigation: Jigsaw | *Now take this time to sort, synthesize and prepare your information. When everyone is ready, you'll regroup to teach each other.* |
| Student A teaches group | *Along the eastern coast. . . .* |
| Student B teaches group | *Did you know . . . ?* |
| Student C teaches group | *Cowboy books, sunshine and sand. . . .* |

## LESSON PLANNER

### Think Abouts . . .

What is an appropriate use? What is an inappropriate use? When might I *overlook* this strategy? Why?

Can I "steal" the idea illustrated in the vignette? Do I want to *duplicate* it?

Is there an existing lesson I can redesign to *replicate* this strategy?

How can I fold this into a lesson I've planned? Does it *integrate* or connect with something I already do?

How can I bridge this into several areas? Where else can I *map* this for additional practice and transfer?

What idea is percolating? Can I *innovate* using some key aspect of this strategy?

### My Lesson Idea

Topic or Unit:____________________________

My purpose for this lesson:

My idea . . . in a nutshell:

Why this strategy seems right:

Other thoughts:

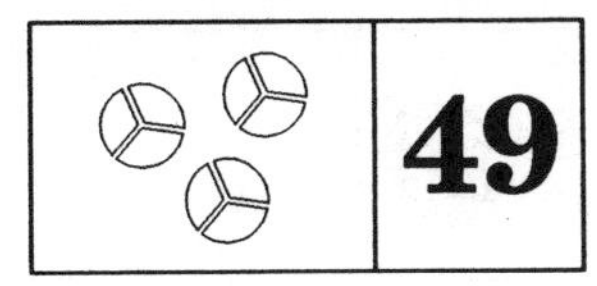


## DOUBLE-ENTRY JOURNAL: PROCESSING

| Description of the Lesson | Reflections on the Lesson |
| --- | --- |
| **What I did before the lesson:** | **Thoughts, ideas, connections I'm making . . .** |
| **What I did during the lesson:** | |
| **What I did following the lesson:** | |

## QUICK REFERENCE OF COOPERATIVE INTERACTIONS

| Design | Symbol | Explanation |
|---|---|---|
| #1 Lecture/Rhetorical Questioning: Teacher Talk (Perhaps Professor Kingsfield) | 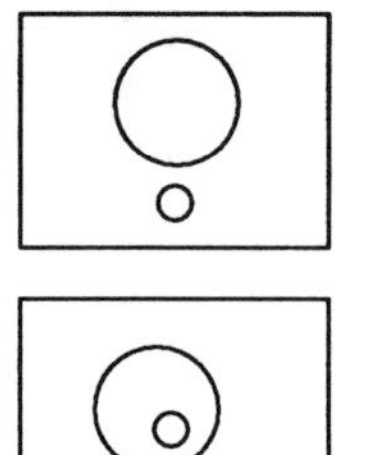 | Stand-up teaching, lecturing to whole class. |
| #2 Signals/Direct Questioning: Surveying (Hunter) | | Lecturing to class, interrupting for signals by group or for answer by one student. |
| #3 Turn To Your Partner And. . . (TTYPA) (Weaver & Cotrell) | 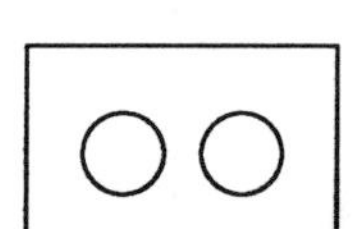 | Informal sharing by partners in which interaction is brief and quick. |
| #4 Paired Partners: Think Aloud (Bloom; Whimbey) | 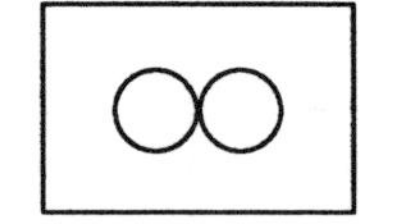 | One partner reflecting the thinking of the other partner who is talking aloud as he thinks through a problem. |
| #5 Dyads: Think/Pair/Share (Lyman & McTighe) | 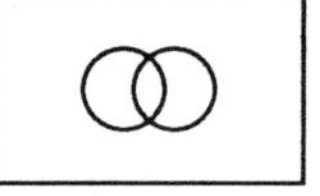 | Partners first thinking alone and then sharing ideas—sometimes coming to one idea for their pair. |
| #6 Triads: Observer Feedback (Costa; Rowe) | 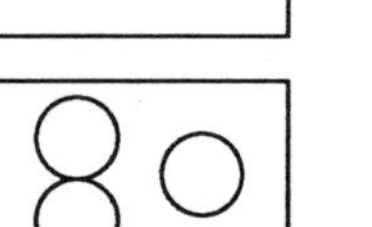 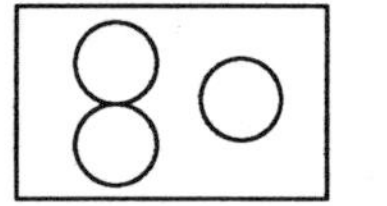 | Partner interaction enhanced by objective observer feedback. |
| #7 Tell/Retell: 2-4-8 (Fogarty & Bellanca) | 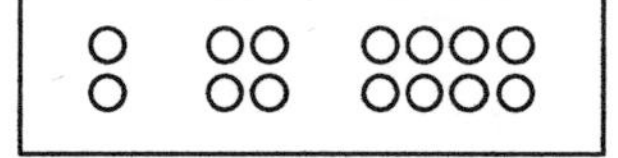 | Two people telling ideas; two sets of two retelling their partners' ideas, a group of eight retelling all ideas. |
| #8 Cooperative Learning: Groups (Johnson & Johnson; Kagan; Slavin) | 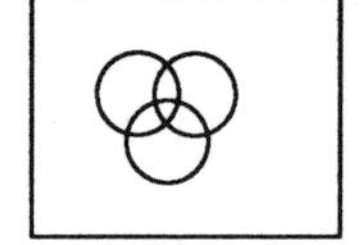 | Small groups of three students working interdependently, but all members accountable for all the work. |
| #9 Traveling Clusters: People Search (Workshop Leaders) | 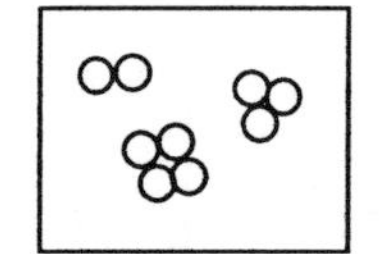 | Students moving from group to group, forming informal clusters as they share information and gather signatures. |
| #10 Forced Response: Wraparound (Howe & Howe) | 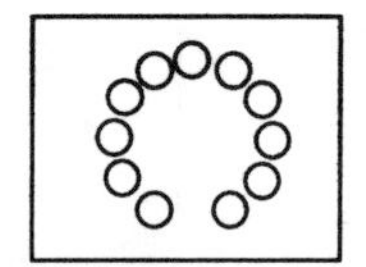 | Round-robin style, students responding in turn to a lead-in statement cued by the teacher. |
| #11 Total Group Response: Human Graph (Fogarty) | 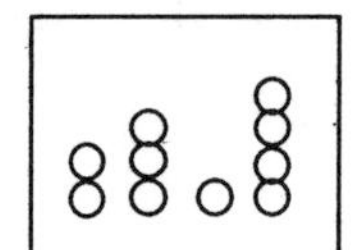 | Students lining up on an imaginary graph to indicate their preferences. |
| #12 Group Investigation: Jigsaw (Aronson; Sharan & Sharan) | 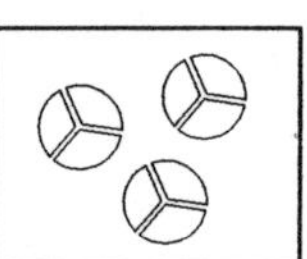 | In groups of three, each member researching a third of the group work and then teaching it to the others in the threesome. |

# AFTERWORD

## The New School "Lecture"

Based on the best research and the best practices, the cooperative interaction designs that distinguish the new school "lecture" from the traditional seem to offer a positive and optimistic prognosis for future use in our classrooms. By their very nature, cooperative learning strategies create a bubbling-up effect among both students and teachers, somehow producing an energy that is at once contagious and self-propelling.

Anyone using cooperative interactions in the classroom attests to the fact that once begun, the positive effects on student motivation, achievement and self-concept are so immediately visible and so astonishingly dramatic that novices are extrinsically motivated to do more. That's why cooperative learning is sprouting in the schools at the grass-roots level.

The designs for thoughtful interactions described in this book provide a vigorous repertoire of instructional strategies. The seasoned practitioner appropriately selects from these strategies as opportunities occur in the instructional arena.

By varying the types of interactions and creating designs or variations on the themes presented, teachers provide a myriad of social learning experiences for students. In turn, students reveal both their thinking paradigms and their social skills as they become involved and responsible for their own learning.

The old lecture, according to Gould, is "an occasion when you numb one end to benefit the other"; the new school lecture resembles a conversation. In a conversation, as Armour suggests, "it is all right to *hold* the conversation for a time, but you should let go of it now and then." The new school lecture sees the teacher skillfully "holding" student attention and at the same time "letting go" of center stage to invite thoughtful and engaging student conversation.

# BIBLIOGRAPHY

**General**

Ferguson, M. (1980). *The aquarian conspiracy.* Los Angeles: J.P. Tarcher.

Fuller, R. Buckminster. (1981). *Critical path.* New York: St. Martin's Press.

Goodlad, J. (1984). *A place called school.* New York: McGraw-Hill Book Company.

Peters, T. and Waterman, R., Jr. (1982). *In search of excellence.* New York: Warner Communications.

**Lecture/Rhetorical Questioning: Teacher Talk**

Weaver, R. and Cotrell, H. (Summer 1986). Using interactive images in the lecture hall. *Educational Horizons,* 64:4, pp. 180-185.

**Signals/Direct Questioning: Surveying**

Hunter, M. (1983). *Reinforcement.* El Segundo, CA: TIP Publications.

**Turn To Your Partner And...(TTYPA)**

Weaver, R. and Cotrell, H. (Summer 1986). Using interactive images in the lecture hall. *Educational Horizons,* 64:4, pp. 180-185.

**Paired Partners: Think Aloud**

Bloom, B. and Broder, L. (1950). *Problem solving process of college students.* Chicago: University of Chicago Press.

Whimbey, A., and Whimbey, L. (1975). *Intelligence can be taught.* New York: Innovative Science.

**Dyads: Think/Pair/Share**

Lyman, F. and McTighe, J. (April, 1988). Cueing thinking in the classroom: The promise of theory-embedded tools. *Educational Leadership,* 45:7.

Whimbey, A., and Whimbey, L. (1975). *Intelligence can be taught.* New York: Innovative Science.

**Triads: Observer Feedback**

Bellanca, J. and Fogarty, R. (1990). *Blueprints for thinking in the cooperative classroom.* Palatine, IL: Skylight Publishing, Inc.

Costa, A. (1986). *Teaching for intelligent behavior.* Unpublished Syllabus (3rd Edition).

Rowe, M. B. (1969). Science, silence and sanctions. *Science and Children.* 6, pp.11-13.

**Tell/Retell 2-4-8**

Fogarty, R. and Opeka, K. (1988). *Start them thinking.* Palatine, IL: Skylight Publishing, Inc.

**Cooperative Learning: Groups**

Bellanca, J. and Fogarty, R. (1990). *Blueprints for thinking in the cooperative classroom.* Palatine, IL: Skylight Publishing, Inc.

Johnson, R. and Johnson D. (1986). *Circles of learning: Cooperation in the classroom.* Alexandria, VA: ASCD.

Kagan, S. (1988). *Cooperative learning: Research for teachers.* Riverside, CA: University of California.

Sharan, S. and Sharan, Y. (1976). *Small group teaching.* Englewood Cliffs, NJ: Educational Testing Publications.

Slavin, R. E. (1983). *Cooperative learning.* New York: Longman.

**Traveling Clusters: People Search**

Fogarty, R. and Bellanca, J. (1987). *Patterns for thinking: Patterns for transfer.* Palatine, IL: Skylight Publishing, Inc.

**Forced Response: Wraparound**

Fogarty, R. and Bellanca, J. (1987). *Patterns for thinking: Patterns for transfer.* Palatine, IL: Skylight Publishing, Inc.

Howe, L. and Howe, M. (1975). *Personalizing education: Values clarification and beyond.* New York: Hart.

**Total Group Response: Human Graph**

Fogarty, R. and Bellanca, J. (1987). *Patterns for thinking: Patterns for transfer.* Palatine, IL: Skylight Publishing, Inc.

Johnson, N. L. (1990). *Questioning makes the difference.* Beavercreek, OH: Pieces of Learning/Creative Learning Consultants.

Bellanca, J. and Fogarty, R. (1986). *Catch them thinking* (4th Edition). Palatine, IL: Skylight Publishing, Inc.

**Group Investigations: Jigsaw**

Aronson, E. (1978). *The jigsaw classroom.* Beverly Hills, CA: Sage Publications.

Sharan, S. and Sharan, Y. (1976). *Small group teaching.* Englewood Cliffs, NJ: Educational Testing Publications.

**Transfer of Learning**

Beyer, B.K. (1987). *Practical strategies for the teaching of thinking.* Boston: Allyn & Bacon.

Joyce, B.R. and Showers, B. (1983). *Power in staff development through research and training.* Alexandria, VA: ASCD.

Perkins, D.N. and Salomon, G. (September 1988). Teaching for transfer. *Educational Leadership*. pp. 22-32.

Perkins, D.N. and Salomon, G. (January-February 1989). Are cognitive skills context bound? *Educational Researcher*. pp. 22-32.

# NOTES

# NOTES

There are
one-story intellects,
two-story intellects, and three-story
intellects with skylights. All fact collectors, who
have no aim beyond their facts, are one-story men. Two-story men
compare, reason, generalize, using the labors of the fact collectors as
well as their own. Three-story men idealize, imagine,
predict—their best illumination comes from
above, through the skylight.

*—Oliver Wendell
Holmes*